The Mountains of Canada

The Mountains of Canada

Randy Morse / Introduction by Andy Russell

The Mountaineers

Published by The Mountaineers,
719 Pike Street, Seattle, WA 98101
ISBN 0-916890-74-0

Published simultaneously in Canada by
Hurtig Publishers, 10560 105 Street,
Edmonton, Alberta

Published simultaneously in Great Britain by
Cordee, 249 Knighton Church Road,
Leicester, England, LE2 3JQ

Printed and bound in Canada

For Ulrika and Andreas

Contents

Introduction

Mountains have always been something of a paradox to man. He has both loved and hated them, prayed to them and cursed them, taken shelter in them and exploited them, conquered them and been defeated by them. He has stood in awe and wonder as he watched a giant peak shrugging the mist off its shoulders to tower in majesty—tall, craggy, and deceptively serene with its spires outlined against the faultless blue of the sky. At other times he has looked at mountains with repugnance. Sometimes he has fled from them, but he has often ventured up their steep flanks, a tiny moving speck contrasting against the snow, before becoming lost from view on the bare rock of minaret or cliff.

Over the centuries, human beings have shared the mountains with eagles, with grizzly bears, wild sheep, and goats; have walked in the splendour of hanging meadows spangled with brilliant flowers; have seen the great wind-twisted trees— gnarled monuments, torture-marked from their battles with lightning storms, avalanches, and hurricanes; have pitched their tents and lit their campfires sheltered among the boulders and timberline trees in some glacier-gouged scar, and been grateful.

But sometimes this delicately balanced relationship has been destroyed by those who bore deep holes into a mountain to rip minerals from its very guts, or who strip its flanks of everything alive; who transform a paradise into a cold, dead desert. Although the mammoth peaks in the cordilleras of the world may seem indestructible, they are in their own way very fragile in the life that they support. Perhaps it is this mix of contrasts that makes them anathema to those who build skyscrapers along the concrete canyons of their cities.

To some, the very grandeur of the mountains represents a threat, for the great peaks are a reminder of our own insignificance. Whether we realize it or not, we are born of the same womb of nature as the mountains, and they offer comparisons measurable in bulk but immeasurable in spirit. Long before the technology of flight was invented, they offered the chance to crawl up to their summits, with sinews straining, and to stand high above drifting clouds and look at horizons never before seen by human eyes. Mountains have helped build both men and women to a physical perfection of muscle and bone, though they have then smashed some of their acolytes to unrecognizable bloody rags.

Mountains are indeed a paradox, and yet they attract climbers as alluringly as sirens beckoning in a gale, enticing travellers toward their rocky peaks. This is especially true of Canada's mountains. Men and women from around the world get a certain look in their eyes when they speak of the Canadian Rockies, of the coastal mountains of British Columbia, and the ice-girdled peaks of the Yukon.

The more adventurous respond to the challenge, prepared to lose themselves in storms, to brave gaping fissures—the greenish-blue, bottomless crevasses—and to climb rock faces where the handholds and footholds on ice-sheathed rock are not much more than figments of the imagination. A few are fated to stay on the mountains forever. Those who come back are never quite the same again. Sometimes they are scarred for life, but generally they are the better for their experiences. They have tasted of the unknown. Their spirits soar: larger, more understanding, and keenly attuned to their world. They make good company round a dancing campfire on a stormy night when the peaks are lost among wind-torn clouds and flying snowflakes. They are very real people with a common bond, regardless of the colour of their skins. They know the meaning of love and true companionship.

It is a shame that here in Canada, where we have so much, we tend to turn our eyes southward from where we live on a relatively narrow strip of land along our southern border. We fail to see the remarkable, and in many ways unique, life quality of our own home. And because we are so rich, and in such a hurry to become richer by a false set of standards, we tend unthinkingly to tear what we want from this great country when we could profit vastly by developing our needs with gentler hands and more understanding minds. Thus, we needlessly destroy our very identity as Canadians and assume a heavy responsibility for actions that will make poor our grandchildren and their children. For this, they may well curse us. Although the mountain giants will still stand, they may be greatly scarred. There can be no worse shame than to have our descendants look back to the stupidity and wastefulness of their ancestors.

The mountains of Canada are a very special heritage—as this book clearly illustrates. They are a national treasure, to be appreciated in the present with joy and wonder, and to be protected thoughtfully for the generations to come.

ANDY RUSSELL
Waterton Park, Alberta,
1978

Preface

In a world fast running out of reminders of the cosmic splendour of this planet at its roughest and most dynamic, the mountains of Canada occupy a very special place. Perhaps nowhere else on earth is there such a profusion of truly wild peaks as there is in this country. And perhaps nowhere else on earth is the contrast between the less appealing side of modern civilization and high, cold, splendidly cruel nature so startlingly sharp.

Clearly, such a magnificent natural heritage places a heavy burden of responsibility on all of us. While our mountains are of little economic value, aside from the minerals they may conceal, they do constitute an important—a globally important—spiritual resource.

For those of us who are afforded the opportunity and the privilege of walking or climbing among them, this point needs no stressing. But even for those who, either by circumstance or choice, will never explore Canada's mountains in a direct and personal way, the very fact that such mountains exist in our world of noise, violence, overpopulation, and increasing pollution offers an immense inspiration. They were. They are. They will continue to be. Or so we hope.

What, then, should you expect to find in these pages? I have included little in the way of geology and very little geography. This is not a travel guide and certainly not a climber's guide. What you will find here are over a hundred superb colour photographs of Canadian mountains—famous mountains, notorious mountains, familiar mountains, and more than a few which you never will have seen or heard of before.

The Mountains of Canada is not intended to be a comprehensive collection. Of the thousands of spectacular peaks in this country, I have selected but a few. There are entire ranges, literally hundreds of beautiful and significant peaks, that have not been included. It was not my intention to create a catalogue, a complete, unabridged Canadian alpine compendium. Rather, what follows should be viewed as a modest and extremely subjective sample of what this country has to offer in the way of high, wild places.

I have concentrated the text almost exclusively on man's highest and most committed encounters with Canada's mountains. Where there were stories to tell, I have told them. But, whenever possible, I have allowed the peaks to speak for themselves, using the lenses of some of the finest photographers in the country to convey their message.

There are a great number of people I would like to thank for helping me, whether directly or indirectly, to put this book together. They include Phil Dowling, Chris Hale, Mel Hurtig, Gary Kirk, Carlotta Lemieux, Jim McMillan, Charlotte Morse, Garfield Morse, Marianne Morse, John Satterburg, and, in particular, the many fine photographers who supplied the pictures that are the real substance of the book.

For those of you who are climbers, I hope that *The Mountains of Canada* will bring back a few pleasant memories of rough rock, scratched and swollen fingers, intense comradeship, ice and air, and vast panoramas of the earth as it used to be; of mountains climbed, of mountains to be climbed, and (perhaps best of all) of mountains only to be dreamed of. For those of you who simply appreciate magnificent scenery, here is a massive helping of it. And for those who long for adventure in a world gone soft, lazy, and self-indulgent, this book is, most especially, for you.

RANDY MORSE
Edmonton, 1978

The Mountains of Canada

A tremendous view opened in front of our eyes—there, still two large glacier-filled valleys away, stood our mountain—a huge, long, massive wall, strong, dominating, inspiring awe rather than admiration in its beauty.

George Lowe, mountaineer, on first seeing Mount Alberta

Mount Alberta is one of the most threatening, seemingly cheerless mountains in Canada. Its walls are stolidly uncompromising; its rock dark and treacherously friable. Long after the other major peaks of the main range of the Rockies had been climbed, the summit of Alberta remained untrodden.

It was not until 1925 that the mountain was climbed, by a Japanese-Swiss party. The group was led by Yuko Maki and consisted of five other Japanese climbers as well as the guides Hans Kohler and Heinrich Fuhrer, and Swiss amateur Jean Weber.

The climbers met in Jasper, then travelled up the Athabasca Valley, turning east up Habel Creek. From a high camp established near the southeast base of the mountain, they made their assault via the southeast face on July 21st. The ascent took longer than expected. It was 7:35 P.M. and nearly dark when the top was reached, forcing the entire group to spend a crowded night clustered on the narrow summit ridge, described by Fred Ayres, a member of the second ascent party, in the following way:

> The view which greeted us was disheartening. As far as we could see through the fog the ridge was dangerously narrow, with precipitous drops on both sides, and consisted of a series of little notches and shattered pinnacles.

All went well despite the airy bivouac. Alberta climbed, the Japanese returned to their homeland, leaving behind a memento of their accomplishment which was soon to take on legendary proportions. Maki had left an ice axe on the summit, an axe which bore the initials of the expedition's Japanese patron. In no other way was the axe extraordinary. Over the ensuing years, very few climbers succeeded in duplicating the 1925 first ascent. Perhaps as a result of Mount Alberta's growing reputation as one of the fiercest challenges in the Rockies, Maki's axe gradually became silver-plated, then, through the metaphysics of imagination, solid gold!

The first Canadian ascent of Alberta, the third overall, was not made until 1958 when a party led by Hans Gmoser repeated the Japanese route. In fact, only one other major route has been established on the peak, via the forbidding north face. I. Glidden and George Lowe reached the top after struggling two days and nights with steep ice and even steeper rotten rock. In all, Alberta's north face ranks as one of the most impressive alpine climbs yet established in the Rockies.

Opposite: Tucked well out of sight in the Columbia Icefields region, **Mount Alberta** (11,874 feet/3,619 metres) is one of the most uncompromising peaks in the main range of the Rockies.

O Canada's mountains are rugged and tall,
      So many there are you can't count them all,
Their glaciers and snows touch the sky's azure blue,
      Their sheer rock cliff-sides reflect every hue,
Their magnificent summits—all corniced snow—
      Look down on the green wooded valleys below.
There's no place on earth where I'd rather be
      For Canada's mountains are heaven to me.

Lynda R. Woods

Opposite: The upper reaches of the northwest shoulder of **Mount Andromeda** (11,300 feet/3,444 metres), a popular peak with several challenging snow and ice routes located near the Banff-Jasper Highway in the Columbia Icefields area.

Right: The snow-draped summit of **Mount Archibald** in the Yukon's Kluane Range. Here the north face is seen at sunset.

19

Once every few months we had both climbed a big wall; either in Yosemite, Norway, or in the Alps, and the craving to go on was never satisfied. This was to be our biggest route in terms of size, remoteness and weather problems. We were within a stone's throw of a supreme test of our abilities. To apply one's best techniques, to suffer miserable wet cold conditions, to go on when every muscle ached, to forge up despite a strong logical inner will to go back down. But also to experience that heightening of sensory perception that such suffering induces and to experience the inner calm that springs from having accomplished an exhilarating climb.

Doug Scott, before attempting the ascent of Mount Asgard

Mount Asgard (6,600 feet/2,012 metres) is a strikingly impressive granite peak located on Baffin Island's Cumberland Peninsula, near Pangnirtung Fjord in the eastern Arctic. Asgard's north peak was first ascended in 1953 by an Arctic Institute of North America party. The south summit was first scaled in 1971 by a party led by Doug Scott.

The sheer rock walls, unpredictable weather, and remote setting make virtually any climb of Asgard a significant achievement, in many ways comparable with a climb of, for example, Patagonia's Fitzroy. The west face of Asgard is undoubtedly one of the most awe-inspiring rock walls in the western hemisphere.

Opposite above: Baffin Island's twin-summited **Mount Asgard** seen from the Freya-Asgard Col looking northeast down the King's Parade Glacier.

Opposite below: **Mount Asgard** seen from the northeast end of Glacier Lake, looking over the Turner Glacier.

Night's candles are burnt out, and jocund day
Walks tiptoe on the misty mountain tops.

William Shakespeare, *Romeo and Juliet*

The north face of British Columbia's **Mount Assiniboine,** powdered with alpenglow. This awesome face was first climbed in 1967 by the Anglo-American trio of Yvon Chouinard, Chris Jones, and Joe Faint.

Opposite: A classic view of **Mount Assiniboine,** draped in a swirl of cloud, seen from the shores of Lake Magog.

The towering pyramid of Mount Assiniboine (11,870 feet/3,618 metres) challenges the observer's ability to comprehend the incomprehensible and makes man's puny attempts at plagiarism seem laughable.

As with no other peak in this country, Assiniboine and Canada have become synonymous. When seen at a distance, Assiniboine exudes an elegance, a cleanness of line and a symmetry of form rivalled by few other mountains in the world. At close quarters, however, the shape, form, and character of the peak change dramatically. The impression of firmness and airy solidity gives way to the crumbling reality of black, loose, sedimentary rock. Elegant lines disappear, dwarfed or blocked out by bands and bulges of friable stone interlaced with veins of ice and snow. Yet even when one curses the precarious handholds and footholds or the treacherously ice-glazed rock, the knowledge that one is climbing Assiniboine somehow makes it all easy to accept, even enjoy. A climb, *any* climb, of Assiniboine is a very special climb indeed.

Mount Assiniboine was first ascended in 1901, via the southwest face, by the British mountaineer Sir James Outram and the Swiss guides Christian Bohren and Christian Hasler.

Assiniboine's northwest face, the most popular line of ascent, in the sun.

Opposite: **Assiniboine** at rest, seen from Sunburst Lake.

The sane friends of the mountaineer always regard him with mixed feelings, compounded mainly of good-natured tolerance and pity.

J.A. Cory

Mount Athabasca (11,452 feet/3,491 metres) is a thoroughly agreeable peak that looms over the Banff-Jasper Highway at the Columbia Icefields, directly across from the Icefields Chalet.

It was first climbed in 1898 by J. Norman Collie and Herman Wooley, both of whom were destined to become presidents of the British Alpine Club. From the top, the two men witnessed a sight no human had before seen:

> The view that lay before us in the evening light was one that does not often fall to the lot of modern mountaineers. A new world was spread at our feet; to the westward stretched a vast icefield probably never before seen by human eye, and surrounded by entirely unknown, unnamed, and unclimbed peaks. From its vast expanse of snows the Saskatchewan Glacier takes its rise, and it also supplies the headwaters of the Athabasca; while far away to the west, bending over in those unknown valleys glowing with evening light, the level snows stretched, to finally melt and flow down more than one channel into the Columbia River, and thence to the Pacific Ocean.

Although the excitement of the first ascent has long since been removed, one of the most rewarding features of a climb of Athabasca remains the superb view.

Opposite above: The north face of **Mount Athabasca,** seen from the summit ridge.

Opposite below: **Mount Athabasca,** in early summer.

The St. Elias Range's **Mount Augusta** and **Mount St. Elias** are two of the mightiest mountains on the North American continent.

Hark! fast by the window
The rushing winds go,
To the ice-cumbered gorges,
The vast seas of snow!
There the torrents drive upward
Their rock-strangled hum;
There the avalanche thunders
The hoarse torrent dumb.
I come, O ye mountains!
Ye torrents, I come!

Matthew Arnold, "Parting"

Mount Augusta (14,070 feet/4,289 metres) and Mount St. Elias (18,008 feet/5,489 metres) are two of the giants straddling the Yukon-Alaska border in the St. Elias Range.

Augusta, named for the wife of Professor I.C. Russell, who opened the route to Mount St. Elias in 1891, was first climbed on July 4th, 1952, by American Pete Schoening's party via the north face and north ridge, a difficult climb involving considerable step cutting and delicate ice climbing.

Mount St. Elias was probably first seen by a European in 1741, when Sven Waxel, captain of the ship *St. Peter,* one of Vitus Bering's two ships of discovery, spied an enormous snow peak to the northeast. A cape was named after the patron saint of the day — St. Elias.

In 1778, Captain James Cook ascribed an altitude of 18,100 feet to the mountain — only ninety-two feet off the mark! However, it was not until 1891 that anyone actually reached St. Elias. In that year, Professor Russell approached the mountain via an arm of the Malaspina Glacier. The professor eventually reached Russell Col, pushing on to an elevation of over 4,400 metres on the northeast shoulder of St. Elias before turning back. From this point Russell became the first to gaze on the vast Seward Glacier and he was also the first person to see the towering Mount Logan in its entirety.

Six years after the Russell expedition, one of the greatest climbing *gestalts* in history landed at Malaspina Beach near Point Manby, intent on climbing Mount St. Elias. The party was Italian. Its leader: the Duke of Abruzzi. Having reached the mountain, he established a high camp at 3,749 metres. The following day, after nine hours of climbing, the entire expedition successfully gained the summit — an incredible achievement. It was not until some sixty years had gone by that the major peaks seen by the duke and his party from the summit of St. Elias were to be climbed.

*Take the woman whose usual occupation is a sedentary one...
put her on the train and send her to the mountains. The imperfect glimpses of this peak and that gorge are small foretastes of what she is going to enjoy, for no one knows the mountains who sees them only from the car window. Now she has reached her destination and is left to exchange for the rattle of the train the music of rushing torrents, to breathe in the keen pure air which finds its way to the very last air-cell of her lungs, and to rest her tired eyes on beauties of form and colour never before imagined.*

Mary E. Crawford, turn-of-the-century Canadian climber

Opposite: **Mount Aurora** (9,350 feet/2,850 metres) forms the west buttress of Marvel Pass, near Mount Assiniboine in eastern British Columbia. Aurora was first climbed by members of the Boundary Commission in 1916.

People who have never done any climbing have since asked me how I enjoyed the glorious view which unfolded before me as we went up. I have been forced to draw upon my imagination for a reply to this question. As a matter of fact, all I saw on the way up Huber were Edouard's boots. They pervaded the whole landscape and rose and fell with the regularity of clockwork. Occasionally, very occasionally, these boots were near enough to be studied in detail, but more often I had to content myself with mere impressionistic glimpses of them disappearing upwards, ever upwards.

Ethel Jones, early Canadian climber, describing one of her first ascents

Opposite: The south ridge of **Mount Balfour** (10,734 feet/3,272 metres), a peak located eight kilometres north of Yoho National Park's Takakkaw Falls. Balfour was first climbed in 1898 by the Reverend Charles L. Noyes, Charles Thompson, and G.M. Weed (whom Hugh Stutfield referred to as "a true son of America," due to his ability to sleep without recourse to cork mattress or bedstead, "wrapped only in his blanket and ground sheet").

Upon rounding a bastion at the point where we came to the edge of the snowfield. . . it was evident that we should succeed in getting to the top, but from the saddle itself we had our first view of the actual summit, which too evidently was upon the cornice overhanging the northerly face of the mountain. The extent of the overhang and the probable security of the huge cornice were carefully noted, and as soon as the final climb up the rounded side of the snowfield lying above us was made, we were happily congratulating one another upon having accomplished the first ascent of Mt. Ball.

John D. Patterson, member of the first ascent party, 1907

Below: The east face of **Mount Ball** (10,865 feet/3,312 metres). A steep, glacier-studded rock wall over 1,200 metres high, it is located on the Continental Divide near Vermilion Pass.

*Go carefully lads, be careful; a single moment's enough to make
one dead for the whole of one's life.*

J. Pecoste, guide; advice to young climbers

Mount Blane (9,820 feet/2,993 metres) is one of the premier summits of the Opal Range, a cluster of steep peaks with generally sound rock, located near the Kananaskis River not far from Banff townsite. Here, its north ridge is seen from nearby Mount Hood. Blane was first ascended in 1955 by the Alberta climbers Gerry Johnson, David Kennedy, and Pat Duffy. Frank Koch, the fourth member of the party, was killed when struck by a falling rock while ascending a prominent gully on the northwest face.

The Northeast Face soared sheer above, giving it the appearance of a huge medieval fortress, a succession of rock buttresses and ice fields that rose tier upon tier to the pure white peak above. At this end a marvellous tower stood smooth and gleaming in the sun, the summit tapering to a sharp point. This was called Breidablick, the palace of Baldr.

Dave Sellars, on his expedition to Baffin Island's Pangnirtung area

The two-in-one massif of **Breidablick-Baldr** (approx. 6,000 feet/1,829 metres) is one of the most impressive peak clusters in an altogether impressive area — the Pangnirtung region of Baffin Island's Cumberland Peninsula.

A wall built of unmortared bricks by a gang of untutored work-men.

Frank Smythe's description of Mount Brussels

While Frank Smythe certainly must be regarded as one of the more important figures on the Canadian climbing scene in the 1940s and 1950s, his comments on the insignificance of Mount Brussels must be taken with an Everest-sized grain of salt. But he had his reasons for this apparent lack of appreciation for one of the most challenging peaks in the Rockies.

When seen from a distance, Mount Brussels does indeed appear rather insignificant, a mere stone blemish on the shoulder of Mount Christie. To be confronted with Brussels at close quarters is quite another matter. Steep, often overhanging on all sides, Brussels is one of those comparatively rare peaks that does not offer at least one easy means of access to its summit. As a result, Brussels was not even attempted until 1930. In that year, the Hainworth-Strumia party, which had just made the first ascent of nearby Christie, launched what proved to be a futile assault.

Throughout the remainder of the thirties and well into the forties, Brussels continued to repel every attempt launched against it. Some of the finest climbers in North America were stopped cold, including Rex Gibson, Fred Beckey — and also Frank Smythe.

The climbing history of Brussels reveals a major shift in the direction and even the morality of Canadian climbing, moving from the largely English tradition of man (stripped of all but his own will to overcome) against mountain, to the German/American school of modern high-angle, highly technical climbing.

Frank Smythe represented the former school. He considered that mountaineering, the noblest of all sports, should be a one-on-one match-up between climber and mountain. According to the hoary rules governing this very serious game, the mountain had at its disposal all the usual weapons: avalanche, rockfall, bergschrund, white-out, holdless slabs, overhangs, verglas, and moraine. To combat these obstacles, the climber was allowed only a limited selection of tools: boots, ice axe, rope, and crampons. Nothing else.

Thus, with the odds seemingly stacked from the beginning in favour of the mountain, when a climber did succeed, it was always clear that this constituted a triumph of humanity in the raw over nature similarly clad. And when a climber failed, he knew precisely where to place the blame.

This approach began to be undermined in the early 1930s when young mountaineers from Austria and Germany, making use of the latest in technical climbing equipment, blazed new routes previously considered unclimbable. The English and Canadians generally condemned this new trend and, in fact, in some cases went so far as to equate the new, extreme school with fascism.

Against this philosophical backdrop Smythe approached Brussels in 1947, fully intending to succeed or fail without recourse to hammer, piton, and carabiner. He failed, as it turned out, stopped by an overhang made treacherous by dangerously loose rock.

The next year, Brussels was finally climbed by Ray Garner and Jack ("Jiggs") Lewis, two chubby Americans, sporting felt hats with feathers jauntily stuck in the brims and short Eisenhower-style climbing jackets. Smythe and many other climbers in Canada were outraged: the two had used both pitons and expansion bolts to reach the top. Garner later described how he and Lewis had managed to overcome the overhanging section that had thwarted Smythe:

> We placed a tamp-in (i.e. an expansion bolt) for belay near the base of this
> pitch. I led out on a diagonal traverse to a small ledge about 40 feet from

the starting point. An insecure piton gave some degree of protection while I drilled a hole for another tamp-in. Anchored to this tamp, I belayed Jiggs up to the small ledge where we both sat and rested. The ledge was barely large enough to support us, and the exposure made us feel like flies on a wall.

Upon learning of this ascent—and, more importantly, how it had been carried out—Smythe made it clear that as far as he was concerned Brussels remained unclimbed. His comments bear repeating:

> Supposing it was the regular thing for all mountaineers to use pitons on their climbs, would it not be a sign of the degeneracy of man? Would it not mean that he had no longer a desire to risk himself, no longer a spirit of enterprise and initiative?

It is interesting to note that while most serious climbers in this country would have laughed at these words before the end of the 1960s, today the tendency among serious mountaineers gravitates towards Smythe's position. In many climbing circles in Canada and elsewhere, the use of bolts is strenuously discouraged, the use of pitons frowned upon. To climb free, without the aid of technical devices, is the sought-after goal. When help is needed, however, the use of "nuts" is encouraged, as these do not damage the rock, and they demand a personal commitment and a level of judgement quite beyond that usually necessary for piton placement.

The struggle is no longer to reach a summit at all costs; the object rather is to push one's own personal limits to the utmost, an endeavour which demands that one work with the mountain rather than against it. In the words of Maurice Herzog, "When adventure seems to disappear from around us, we will always know where ultimately to find it again—within ourselves."

Overleaf: **Mount Brussels**
(10,370 feet/3,161 metres)
rises from the shoulder of
Mount Christie near the
Continental Divide.

The soaring mass rose in its entirety from the white plains of the Columbian nevé, its flanks so sheer as to suggest absolute inaccessibility and the corniced crest and icy mantle seeming to overhang the dark green depths of the narrow gorge 8,000 feet beneath the topmost pinnacle.

Sir James Outram, grandson of the British general of Indian Mutiny fame and
the first man to climb Mount Assiniboine (1901); on first sighting Mount Bryce

Above: The north face of
Mount Bryce (11,507
feet/3,507 metres), seen here
in early evening from the
Columbia Icefields, is one of
the classic ice climbs in
Canada. The face is almost
1,000 metres high and was
first climbed in 1972 by
J. Jones and E. Grassmann.

The spectacular Purcell Range of British Columbia, of which Bugaboo Spire is a principal peak, was first explored systematically in 1910 by T.G. Longstaff, Arthur O. Wheeler, Byron Harmon, and Conrad Kain.

Until that time, climbers in the Rockies to the east had gazed longingly at the impressive cluster of rock peaks exploding out of their surrounding ice field. But it was not until the Longstaff party's exploratory journey that the attractiveness of the Bugaboo region was actually brought home. Harmon's photographs in particular stirred a considerable amount of climbing interest in the southern Purcells.

Nevertheless, it was not until a logging road was carved out of the bush six years later from Spillimacheen to the forks of Bugaboo Creek that another group of climbers arrived on the scene. Conrad Kain, the famous Austrian-Canadian guide, was again one of their number. Having established their base camp, they settled on "Peak Number Three" as a likely target for their ascent, and on August 29th, 1916, Conrad Kain and John Vincent, together with Albert MacCarthy and his wife, began to inch their way up the south ridge of "Number Three" — or Bugaboo Spire.

Blessed by a clear sky and a warm sun, the four made rapid progress up the ridge's lower slabs. They encountered good, solid granite, which though occasionally quite steep afforded uniformly interesting climbing. All went well until, near the 3,000-metre level, a major obstacle barred all further upward progress: a massive rock tower, or *gendarme,* which emphatically blocked all access to the upper reaches of the ridge. They dubbed it the "Grand Gendarme" and then began to study it for possible weaknesses. In MacCarthy's words, its base "completely spanned the width of the ridge. Its wall on the west side ran up in prolongation of the mighty cliffs that rose from the glacier far below, and its top edge rose sharply like a horn to the point where it joined the high sheer east wall."

After weighing the various possibilities, Kain shed his pack and began to work his way straight up the face of the tower. Just below the top of the obstruction, the pinnacle became overhanging, threatening to force him out and away from the rock. But by now he was committed. He must either force a route up — and quickly, before the strength in his arms gave out — or fall.

He squirmed his way a few feet upward, delicately inching his feet just a bit higher and making maximum use of several small, diagonal cracks. With his feet as high as he dared place them, he made his move, reaching blindly over the tower's overhanging lip for a hold — any hold. Then his feet swung out from under him, dangling over six hundred metres of space. There was a moment's breathless hesitation. Then, with a grunt, he pulled himself over the edge. Two hours after leaving his anxious companions on the ridge below, the cheerful if somewhat ungrammatical call "I make it!" wafted down the compact folds of granite. The Grand Gendarme had been turned. The way to the summit lay open. Bugaboo Spire was climbed.

Since that initial ascent in 1916, Bugaboo Spire has become a Mecca for enterprising Canadian and foreign rock climbers. The northeast ridge (1958), the west face (1959), the north face (1960), and the east face (1960) have all been climbed by various routes. In fact, Bugaboo Spire and its sister peaks have, if anything, become too popular. Boulder Camp, the usual base for climbers in the area, is so overused and overabused that climbers and hikers for whom a rapport with wilderness is an important and integral part of the appeal of the mountains are urged to place their camps elsewhere.

Opposite: **Bugaboo Spire** (10,450 feet/3,185 metres), one of the principal peaks in the Bugaboo Group of British Columbia's Purcell Range.

Right: Looking down on the famous Grand Gendarme, chief obstacle on **Bugaboo Spire's** south ridge.

Above: **Cascade Mountain** (9,836 feet/2,998 metres), a peak located near Banff townsite, has become a popular rock-climbing centre. Here the cliffs of Cascade are plastered with a layer of new snow after an early spring storm.

Det är något bortom bergen, bortom blommorna och sången,
det är något bakom stjärnor, bakom heta hjärtat mitt.
Hören-något går och viskar, går och lockar mig och beder:
Kom till oss, ty denna jorden den är icke riket ditt!

(There's something beyond the mountains, beyond the flowers
*   and the song,*
There's something behind stars, behind my aching heart.
Listen—something goes and whispers, beckoning me and
*   pleading:*
Come to us, for this earth is not your kingdom, come to us,
*   make a start!)*

Opposite: An incredible sea of peaks stretches out into the distance, making the boundaries separating British Columbia, the Yukon Territory, and Alaska seem almost superfluous. This is the greatest collection of peaks on the continent—the **Coast Range.**

Dan Andersson, Swedish poet and lumberjack

Zippers are the almost universal means of closure even though they sometimes snag the fabric or go off the trolley.

The Seattle Mountaineers, *Mountaineering: The Freedom of the Hills*

Opposite: Overlooking Jasper airfield, **Mount Colin,** at 8,815 feet (2,687 metres) is the highest peak in Jasper National Park's Colin Range. It is an impressively slabby upthrust quite popular with rock enthusiasts, due to its clean lines and ready access. While numerous routes now exist up Colin, that of the first ascent (1947) followed the southeast ridge. The members of this party included Noel Odell, John Ross, and Frank Smythe. It is fascinating to note that during this ascent Smythe used a piton as an aid for the first time in his thirty years of climbing. This act smacks of blasphemy, given Smythe's well-known views on the use of mechanical aids. (See "Brussels Peak" — and note the date of Smythe's attempt!)

A little to the north of this peak, and directly to the westward of Peak Athabasca, rose probably the highest summit in this region of the Rocky Mountains. Chisel-shaped at the head, covered with glaciers and snow, it stood alone, and I at once recognised the great peak I was in search of.

J. Norman Collie, one of the most brilliant early climbers in the Canadian Rockies, the Alps, and the Himalayas

He was afraid that the other members of his club would consider the risk he had taken upon himself hare-brained foolishness. But he was not in the least hare-brained. His artistic mind was able to foresee all the dangers he would have to live through with the eye of imagination; nor did that gift weaken his resolve, it simply sharpened his presence of mind.

Kurt Maix, on Diether Marchart, an outstanding mountaineer of the thirties

The past was wiped out, all that mattered was the future; and the future lay over the snow-plastered, ice-glazed summit-wall.

Heinrich Harrer, Austrian climber and adventurer

The snow-powdered slopes of **Mount Deltaform** (11,235 feet/3,424 metres), or Peak Eight of Banff's Ten Peaks, swoop upward after an early autumn snowfall.

At last, at five o'clock, weary and cold, we came to the rock climb, three hundred feet below the summit. At this unpleasant place there is the choice of the side above the glacier, with two hundred feet of steps to cut in the packed snow, where a slip means a three thousand foot sheer drop; or the choice of going right up the rocks, which is almost as bad.

G. Morris Taylor, describing an early ascent of Mount Edith Cavell

Mount Edith Cavell, named after the heroic World War I nurse, dominates the Jasper townsite area in Alberta's Jasper National Park.

Mount Edith Cavell (11,033 feet/3,363 metres) is the dominant peak of the Jasper area, sandwiched between the south angle formed by the Astoria and Whirlpool rivers, northeast of Verdant Pass.

Originally called Mount Fitzhugh, later known locally as Mount Geikie, (the present name of one of the Tonquin Valley's major summits in the Ramparts Group), this graceful peak received its present name in honour of the famous nurse killed by the Germans as a spy in World War I.

In the summer of 1915, Dr. A.J. Gilmour and Edward W.D. Holway left the Alpine Club of Canada's summer mountaineering camp near Mount Robson and headed for Edith Cavell via Jasper. Bushwhacking up Geikie Creek, the two reached Cavell's west ridge three days after having set out. The morning of August 5th dawned dully, with clouds and blowing snow, but this quickly burned away, leaving clear skies and excellent snow conditions for the attempted ascent. All went well, and three and a half hours after beginning up the ridge, Gilmour and Holway reached the summit. This original line has not become the most popular route on the mountain. That distinction goes to the east ridge route put up in July of 1924 by L. Coolidge, G. Higginson, J.E. Johnson, and A. Streich.

Perhaps the most elegant, the most classically alpine route on Cavell is the north face/east summit variant, which was first climbed by the formidable Anglo-American trio of Yvon Chouinard, Joe Faint, and Chris Jones in July 1967. With a directness of line and purpose, this demanding climb combines all the elements that have come to symbolize modern "mixed" climbing: sustained technical difficulty, steep snow and ice, severe and varied rock problems, route-finding, and objective dangers. It is truly a fine route up an important and lovely mountain.

One of the greatest advantages mountaineering has over other sports is that there is no danger of playing to the gallery, no question of exhibitionism. The greatest benefit comes from the impact, on the minds of students, of the symbolic aspect of mountaineering, the feeling of rising higher and higher, surmounting all obstacles. On a mountain, a mountaineer is always the gainer, even if he does not reach the summit. He has at least gained in the qualities which danger and nature in the raw sharpen. He learns to appreciate the virtue of sacrifice, the value of physical exertion almost beyond human endurance, and above all the spirit of comradeship. Men can have victory without pride, and defeat without 'despair,' unaccompanied by the psychological consequences normally attendant upon victory and defeat when competing with fellow human beings.

The Himalayan Mountaineering Institute Bulletin, 1959

Opposite: The **Eiffel Tower** (10,100 feet/3,078 metres) is an impressive spire located immediately north of Eiffel Peak near Moraine Lake in Banff National Park. First climbed in 1952 by two students from Princeton University, Joe E. Murphy and Thomas A. Mutch, the standard route up the tower is reasonably difficult—but the resultant view is well worth the effort.

Mount Eisenhower, bathed in the last rays of an early autumn sun. Eisenhower lies about thirty kilometres from Banff.

Night came down on the mountains. Below, the rustic notes of the Alpine horn had ceased. Leroux prepared a saucepan of hot drink, while the sausage, bacon, jam and dry cakes circulated. Habrab quoted from his favourite author: "They enjoyed a spicy insecurity." That was how it was. Friendship kept us warm. Then the cigarettes, smoked as we sat half-reclining on our rocky couch, tasted amazingly good.

Gaston Rébuffat, French guide and writer, on a bivouac in the Swiss Alps

One of the chief landmarks of the Rockies, Mount Eisenhower (9,076 feet/2,766 metres) is among the most familiar peaks in Canada. For years, its striking rock towers have served as beacons for climbers from all over the world.

The first ascent of Eisenhower was made in 1926 by L. Grassi and P. Ceruth via the northwest face. A few days after this first climb, Joseph Hickson and Edward Ferry made the ascent via the southeast face. They found the final 250 metres to "consist of vertical cliffs, broken by chimneys with overhanging rocks and which entailed roping off on the descent." On June 5th, 1928, the first solo ascent of Eisenhower was made by John Arnold, a resident of Helsinki, Finland. No one saw or talked with the mysterious Arnold, but his record was found on the summit by the fifth ascent party the next summer.

A good deal of controversy has raged about Eisenhower of late, centring on the mountain's name. There are those who argue that the peak was much better served by its former title, Castle Mountain, but the authorities refuse to budge—Eisenhower it is and Eisenhower it will stay. A tempest in a teapot. The mountain speaks most eloquently for itself. Its own choice of names is clear.

The day had a dream-like quality. We seemed to progress through a world of pure forms where the everyday rhythm was retarded because of the unexpectedly large scale of the landscape.

G.V.B. Cochran, on the pleasures of mountaineering

Mount Fifi (8,600 feet/2,621 metres), like the forgotten skeleton of some gargantuan, war-ravaged Gothic cathedral, rises here in terraced columns from the talus near Mount Louis in Banff National Park.

Yes, we had made an excursion into another world and we had come back, but we had brought the joy of life and of humanity back with us. In the rush and whirl of everyday things, we so often live alongside one another without making any mutual contact. We had learned on the North Face...that men are good and the earth on which we were born is good.

Heinrich Harrer, on the human spinoffs of severe climbing

Opposite: **Mount Forbes**, at 11,852 feet (3,612 metres) the seventh highest mountain in the Canadian Rockies, was first climbed in 1902 via the southwest ridge. Forbes lies near the Banff-Jasper boundary and can be seen from the highway, towering up beyond Mount Outram. Here, a view of the south ridge from near the summit.

Right: Also known by the futuristic name "CR6," **Garonne** (8,650 feet/2,637 metres) is located in Jasper National Park one and a half kilometres south of the better-known Mount Colin. Garonne was first climbed in August 1964 by R.G. Harlow and Hans Schwartz, who approached it from the Colin-Garonne Col.

Mature forest naturally gives climbers a sense of security against avalanches originating within the wooded area. One may so easily forget that enough snow to bury a climber or carry him over a cliff may be just as deadly as an avalanche which strips a whole mountainside.

W.A. Don Munday, the discoverer of Mount Waddington and a veteran climber in the Coast Range

61

To me it is always a moving experience to stand up with a hundred others and sing that grand hymn "Unto the Hills" written in Canada, about Canadian mountains. And it is always a thrill too, to have the newly graduated welcomed in—in the older times with a nearly forgotten cry:

> *Yoho, Yo-ho*
> *We are the people who climb, you know;*
> *Up the mountain through snow and cloud*
> *And then, returning, we shout aloud*
> *Yo-ho, YO-HO.*

Sir Edward Oliver Wheeler, former president of the Alpine Club of Canada

The twin towers of Mount Goodsir (north tower: 11,565 feet/3,525 metres; south tower: 11,686 feet/3,562 metres) were early targets for ambitious climbers at the turn of the century.

It is interesting to compare two reactions to the first ascents of these peaks, which are located in British Columbia at the head of Goodsir Creek. Professor Charles Fay of Tufts College, a member of the first party to climb the south tower, described his climb in the following lyrical manner:

> At about 7,000 feet and at the very base of a spur from the southern higher peak, near to a refreshing rill we found two gnarled firs with ample tops, promising a tolerable shelter in case of a sudden shower, and under these we spread our blankets with good hope for the morrow. The sun set clear, the stars gleamed with joyous brightness, and with such omens we saw ourselves already the victors over the untamed monster at whose feet we dared to lie so serenely.
>
> At eleven o'clock we were on the summit — Goodsir was ours. The repulse of two years before was forgotten, and our affections went out to the graceful peak, no longer a sullen monster, and for the joys of that one glorious "hour" spent on its pure snowy summit, we granted it our love for a lifetime.

Compare this with the reaction of J.P. Forde, who took part in the first ascent of the north tower in 1909:

> The climb was not a particularly exciting one, the long time taken to reach the summit being more on account of the extreme caution with which it was necessary to move than because of any difficulties encountered.

A mountain's beauty and character do indeed lie in the eye of the beholder.

Opposite: British Columbia's **Mount Goodsir,** one of the earliest targets for enterprising nineteenth-century mountaineers.

Here I had a few moments of quiet contemplation of a scene that in its awful solitude has left a deep impression on my memory. Some stones, dislodged as I moved, fell with a grinding sound over the edge, toward a narrow chasm, three thousand feet below. A cold wintry wind made a subdued monotone amongst the inequalities of rough stone and the overhanging cliff, and brought up a dust and brimstone odour from the crushing stones. Opposite was a pinnacled mountain stained red and grey, rent into thousands of narrow gullies or beetling turrets by the wear of ages. It was a vast ruin of nature, a barren mass of tottering walls and cliffs, raising two lofty summits far upwards. Between lay a narrow, secluded valley, so thoroughly enclosed that a small lake in it was still covered by the granular, half-melted ice of last winter.

Walter D. Wilcox, an American climber, describing a scene in the Canadian Rockies around the turn of the century

Mount Hooker, long thought
to be one of the highest
mountains in North America.

For many years, the height of Mount Hooker (10,782 feet/3,286 metres) was thought to be approximately 15,700 feet, based on an estimate made in May 1827 by the intrepid Scottish botanist and explorer, David Douglas. From the summit of Mount Brown, whose height Douglas estimated to be 16,000 feet (its actual height is 9,183 feet!), Douglas commented:

> This peak, the highest yet known in the Northern Continent of America, I feel a sincere pleasure in naming Mt. Brown. . . . A little to the southward is one of nearly the same height, rising into a sharper point. This I named Mt. Hooker, in honour of my early patron the Professor of Botany in the University of Glasgow. This mountain I was unable to climb.

In July of 1924, almost one hundred years after Douglas's journey, Philadelphians Alfred J. Ostheimer, Dr. Max M. Strumia, and J. Monroe Thorington, with the Austrian-Canadian guide Conrad Kain, were able to climb Hooker via the west ridge.

Something hidden. Go and find it.
Go and look behind the Ranges—
Something lost behind the Ranges.
Lost and waiting for you. Go!

Rudyard Kipling, "The Explorer"

A strikingly beautiful mountain, Howse Peak (10,793 feet/3,290 metres) was first climbed by J. Norman Collie, the brilliant British mountaineer, and his companions in 1902, almost as a consolation prize.

From the time in 1898 that he first saw Mount Columbia from the summit of Mount Athabasca (see "Mount Columbia"), Collie had longed to be the first to climb the Rockies' second-highest peak. But Sir James Outram beat him to it. Howse Peak, while a lovely summit, was nonetheless not the mountain Collie had come so far to climb. He returned to England a disappointed man.

Opposite: **Howse Peak,** here clad in a winter covering of snow, is the highest summit of the Waputik Group and forms the eastern buttress of Howse Pass, David Thompson's gateway to the Pacific.

Gay started up using direct aid for the first time. When the two-inch crack ended after ten feet, the move above was very difficult. Gay ran out of fingers and peeled off. Pete caught him easily, so he wasn't hurt, although he had scraped a few layers off his hardhat on the way down. This event, and the falling ice blocks earlier in the day, one of which bounced off my head, reinforced the affection Gay and I have for hardhats. Of course Pete, who won't wear one, was never struck. When we told this to Yvon Chouinard after the climb, he took it as confirming evidence for his belief that hardhats attract rocks.

William C. Knowler, describing the first ascent of the northwest face of Howser Spire's north tower

Opposite: **Howser Spire** (north tower: 11,150 feet/3,399 metres; central tower: 10,850 feet/3,307 metres; south tower: 10,850 feet/3,307 metres) is a huge mountain with three distinct peaks, situated at the eastern head of the Vowell Glacier in British Columbia's Bugaboo Group. There are quite literally dozens of routes up each of the towers, all of them extremely demanding— both technically and physically difficult. The south tower, pictured here, was first climbed in 1941 by the Seattle climbers Lloyd Anderson, Helmy Beckey, Lyman Boyer, and Tom Campbell, via the east face and east ridge.

Most men if not all have a spirit of adventure which needs an outlet. Many of the better-known sports...require a lot of money; but climbing needs nothing more than a pair of gym shoes and some old clothes to start with at least. One of the good things about climbing is that it is possible to enjoy it in any form, from messing about on small practice cliffs, to struggling up a huge Himalayan peak.

Joe Brown, veteran British mountaineer

Mount Hubbard (14,950 feet/4,557 metres), with Mount Weisshorn in the foreground, is an impressive summit located near the United States border in the Yukon's St. Elias Range.

Mount Hubbard was first climbed by Bob Bates, N. Clifford, P. Wood, and Walter A. Wood on July 27th, 1951, as Walter Wood describes:

> On the 27th the party set out towards Mt. Hubbard, gaining altitude rapidly on an ascending traverse of a moderate snow slope. At its top the slope eased into a gentle snowfield on the far side of which a final steep wall defended the ample summit. It was reached at such an early hour, 10:30 A.M., and under such pleasant weather conditions, that the party enjoyed the rarity of truly savouring a sub-Arctic victory.

There used to be so few climbers that it didn't matter where one drove a piton, there wasn't a worry about demolishing the rock. Now things are different. There are so many of us, and there will be more. A simple equation exists between freedom and numbers; the more people, the less freedom. If we are to retain the beauties of the sport, the fine edge, the challenge, we must consider our style of climbing.

Royal Robbins, one of America's—and the world's—premier rock climbers

Rotten rock or not, **Mount Hungabee** seen from a distance, as in this photo of the peak taken just before sunset, is a beautiful mountain.

The loveliest approach to Mount Hungabee (11,447 feet/3,489 metres) is from Banff National Park's Lake O'Hara up to the enchanting Opabin Plateau. One must be dedicated in the extreme, or shockingly short of time, not to linger in this delicate fairyland of thick mosses, multicoloured lichens clinging to massive boulders, and beautifully clear alpine tarns reflecting the surrounding peaks.

The Opabin Plateau is positively Tolkienesque, providing a charming counterpoint to the rocky brashness of Hungabee, a mountain which the legendary climber Val Flynn referred to in 1910 as a peak "like all the others in this district, more dangerous than difficult, requiring very careful selection of a route on account of the very rotten rock."

Overleaf: Late afternoon storm seen from Opabin Plateau near **Mount Hungabee**.

Mountain scenery is the antithesis not so much of the plains as of the commonplace. Its charm lies in its vigorous originality.

Leslie Stephen, nineteenth-century mountaineer

Above: Rugged **Mount Ishbel** (9,540 feet/2,908 metres), just north of the Banff — Lake Louise Highway, was first climbed by a party led by L. Grassi in September 1933 via the southwest ridge. Ishbel's sharply serrated ridges, here powdered by a recent snowstorm, extend for over ten kilometres and at several points exceed 2,700 metres.

Loaded down with gear and with French bread sticking out from our sacks, we had another splash and travelled up to the Montenvers by the train, rubbing shoulders with the tourists. I often wondered what they thought of us. They would stare curiously at our tatty clothing and bulging sacks, but whenever you caught their eye they looked quickly away. We didn't exist in the same world. They looked out of the windows and made wondering noises at the sight of the graceful, aloof spire of the Dru. In a few hours' time we would be lost among the cracks and overhangs invisible to the tourists. They would probably think that we were mad. How could you possibly enjoy and appreciate nature when you were fighting for your life thousands of feet from comfort? Useless to try and explain that that is exactly the time and place when nature is at its most meaningful.

Don Whillans, superb British climber (and plumber), describing an encounter with "normal people" in the French Alps.

Opposite: Looking for all the world like a scene from a Norwegian or New Zealand fjord, **Keele Peak** (8,500 feet/2,591 metres) of the central-eastern Yukon's seldom-visited Hess Mountains is reflected in the still waters of Keele Lake.

74

It is an infernal mountain, cold and treacherous. . . . The risks of getting caught are too great, the margin of strength when men are at great heights is too small. Perhaps it's mere folly to go up again. But how can I be out of the hunt? It sounds more like war than sport, and perhaps it is.

George H.L. Mallory, in a letter written shortly before his disappearance near the summit of Mount Everest

Early in 1965, the Government of Canada named a peak in the Yukon's Icefield Range "Mount Kennedy" after the assassinated American president.

That same year, on March 22nd, a party that included Senator Robert Kennedy and Jim Whittaker (the first American to climb Mount Everest) was flown into a base camp that had been established by an advance group at the foot of Mount Kennedy. On the twenty-fourth, eight climbers, including Robert Kennedy, reached the summit.

The temperature, considering the time of year and the setting (nearly 4,200 metres up in an arctic environment) was perhaps the most remarkable feature of the climb — a balmy -20°C!

Opposite: **Mount Kennedy** (13,905 feet/4,238 metres) in the Yukon's Icefield Range.

A good riding yak is much preferable to the sort of beast one is commonly invited to put one's leg over.

H.W. Tilman, British mountaineer and explorer

In May 1972, the last of the major peaks of the St. Elias Range was climbed when an Alaskan party composed of A. Paige, W. Atwood, K. Hart, and E. Thayer reached the summit of King Peak (16,971 feet/5,173 metres).

The party, seeing little in the way of encouragement from the rather imposing sweep of ice, snow, and rock above their camp at King Col, chose instead to gain the west ridge via a steep and terribly exposed snow slope. Once the ridge was gained, the way lay open to the top, though it demanded considerable caution.

Opposite: Here **King Peak** is seen from a camp at King Col, the saddle between Mount Logan and King Peak in the Yukon's St. Elias Range.

Suddenly I heard the unmistakable scrape and grit of sliding boot-nails and clothes. Above my head, over the edge of the roof to the right, I saw Franz's legs shoot out into space. Time stopped. A shiver, like expectancy, trembled across the feeling of unseen grey wings behind me, from end to end of the cliff.

Geoffrey Winthrop Young, distinguished turn-of-the-century British climber

Towering over Lake Louise, **Mount Lefroy** is one of the classic alpine peaks of the main range of the Canadian Rockies.

Mount Lefroy (11,230 feet/3,423 metres) must be one of the most photographed mountains in Canada, given its position at the head of Lake Louise. On any ordinary summer day, thousands of tourists swarm over the lake's imposing chalet and its immediate environs, ogling the peaks and taking snapshot after snapshot.

Less than one hundred years ago things were different. While there was a chalet at the lake, it was little more than a rustic log hut. There were no crowds. Today's acres of parking lots were then grasslands and swamp. It was from this considerably more pastoral setting that Professor Charles Fay, P.S. Abbot, Charles Thompson, and the Reverend George Little set out to climb Mount Lefroy in the summer of 1896.

From the shoulder at the pass that separates Lefroy from nearby Mount Victoria, the four proceeded up steep slopes of ice broken by the occasional band of unstable rock. Late in the afternoon, not far from the summit, they came up against an especially wicked-looking buttress. Rather than waste precious time in traversing around it, they decided to have a go at scaling it directly. Abbot led, unroping so as to allow his companions to stay out of the way of the stonefall he was bound to cause.

As he moved up and out of sight, the other three climbers must have felt that all was well—the top would soon be theirs. Suddenly, all such thoughts were dashed, as Abbot's body hurtled past their horrified eyes, on its way to a fatal meeting with the snow and rocks waiting patiently 275 metres below. The others turned back. Lefroy remained unclimbed.

The next year Professor Fay returned, bringing with him a large and extremely strong party, which included the Swiss guide Peter Sarbach and the redoubtable British climber J. Norman Collie. All went well. From the pass (which had by now been named after the unfortunate Abbot), they climbed steadily upward. When, still quite early in the day, they came to the rock band that had proved the undoing of the previous year's attempt, they simply avoided it by taking to the snow and were soon on the summit. The year 1896 saw a pass tragically named. The year 1897 saw Mount Lefroy successfully climbed.

No ripple of worry from the outside world could touch us. . . . It was hard to go from that beautiful place, to leave the little lake to the butterflies, the gophers, the ducks, the bears and the flowers.

Mary Schäffer, a Pennsylvanian Quaker, recalling an idyllic scene near the Columbia Icefields

The Lieutenants, at 10,550 feet (3,216 metres), form the southwest retaining wall of the Lake of the Hanging Glaciers, seen here in the foreground. The lake is remarkable in that its southern end is covered by a glacier fed by constant avalanches from the hanging glaciers towering above it. This is one of the loveliest and most spectacular areas in British Columbia's interior ranges.

The great mountains, wherein sublimity so much excells our daily things, that in their presence experience dissolves, and we seem to enter upon a kind of eternity.

Hilaire Belloc

Mount Logan, at 19,850 feet (6,050 metres) Canada's highest mountain, has been called "an overture in stone and ice." It is much more than that. Logan is a rolling, thundering, cacophonic symphony of vast faces and endless ridges, all rising to a sustained alpine fortissimo unparalleled in North America—perhaps in the world.

From the base of the Seward Glacier, Logan thrusts upward over four kilometres of Canadian countryside, nudging the sky with its twenty-four kilometre-long summit ridge. Fourteen and a half of those kilometres are over five thousand metres high. Its ridges are virtually incomprehensible, their extent impossible to gauge from a mere photograph. Suffice it to say that one of the ridges stretches a full thirteen kilometres from base to summit.

Without question, Logan is one of the world's most massive mountains. It is also one of the world's tallest when measured from its lowest point to its highest. A Mount Robson standing alongside this Queen of the Yukon would appear to be little more than a foothill, for all its size and dignity. Yet Logan is an elusive peak, visible only from great distances at certain points in the Yukon interior and from a few kilometres of shoreline near Alaska's Yakutat Bay.

Because of its vast size and its tremendously isolated position, climbs of Logan have always had a certain epic quality about them. The first ascent certainly set the stage in this regard.

In late 1924, the Alpine Club of Canada drew up plans for an elaborate expedition to Logan. Albert MacCarthy and H.F. Lambart, on loan from Ottawa's Department of the Interior, were selected as leader and assistant leader. The stage was set for one of the most gruelling and dogged ascents in the history of North American mountaineering.

Based on data collected by the remarkable survey teams of the International Boundary Commission, it was clear to the ACC party that the crux of their climb would involve forcing a passage up the huge icefall which tumbled down the mountain's west face. They achieved this successfully and were able to establish an advance base camp at King Col, a 4,050-metre-high saddle at the top of the trough separating King Peak from Logan's upper slopes. From King Col, the route to the top appeared obvious—a technically easy jaunt up gently undulating glacial slopes to a height of 5,500 metres, then along the ridge to the summit—wherever that might be. But bitterly cold weather and frightful snow conditions were to transform what appeared to be a simple job of putting one foot in front of the other into a harrowing experience that brought several of the expedition's climbers to the very brink of extinction.

After several days of struggling through deep, loose snow, the climbers reached the upper slopes of Logan at about the 5,600-metre level on June 17th, 1925. At this height, they were breathing shallowly, taking only a few steps before stopping to gasp again for air, and one can only imagine their exhausted disappointment when they discovered, after having come so far, that the summit still lay some ten kilometres away.

What to do? The weather made up their minds for them, as it often does in the mountains. Violent winds and –45°C temperatures drove them back to the camp at King Col, where they remained, trapped in their violently flapping tents, until June 21st. Then, with some sign of at least a temporary clearing in the weather, six climbers left the col: MacCarthy, Lambart, and A. Carpe (the American Alpine Club's representative), W.W. Foster (then President of the Canadian Alpine Club), Andy Taylor, a rugged mountain man from McCarthy, Alaska, and N.H. Read, an American climber from Massachusetts. This time they managed to establish a high camp at 5,600 metres.

What followed may best be described as a nightmare, a nightmare which few people have experienced — and survived. On the twenty-second, the six left their high camp and cut the distance to the summit in half. The following day, at 10 A.M., they set out again. Six and a half hours later they had done it. The summit was theirs! But wait....One of them looked up into the wind, then along the ridge. There, two and a half kilometres to the east, lay a point obviously higher than their own position.

There was no question of turning back. They had come too far, risked too much, given too much of themselves to stop short now, within sight of that elusive summit. So they plunged on, their beards frozen solid, their clothes stiff, icy, armoured. With each step they took, the storm, which by now was raging, worsened. By 8:30 P.M. it had become a full-fledged blizzard, and they were right in the middle of it. But for a moment that didn't matter, for suddenly they realized that they had come to a point higher than anything around them. They had finally reached the summit of Logan, the Roof of the Dominion. Canada, unknowing and largely uncaring, lay at their feet.

There was little time for jubilation. It would be an empty victory if they were all to perish after having reached their goal, à la Scott at the South Pole. Turning away from the top, they headed back towards King Col, their tents, and safety. Soon after leaving the summit, the two ropes of three of the climbers became separated in the storm. Albert MacCarthy, together with his companions Foster and Carpe, were forced to bivouac twice, without tent or sleeping bags and wearing clothing that no modern climber would consider suitable for an autumn walk in the park, let alone at an altitude of over five thousand metres in a blizzard. Somehow, they survived. Forty-four hours after their departure, they stumbled into their high camp, exhausted, emaciated, and half-frozen, but alive.

This first ascent of Mount Logan, though lesser known, must rank as a feat of determination, daring, courage, and yes, luck, on a par with Herman Buhl's incredible solo climb of Nanga Parbat or the remarkable American descent from the summit of Everest in 1963.

This doughty Alpine Club party was not to be the only collection of imaginative and determined climbers to approach Logan. In 1959, an all-Canadian expedition under the leadership of Hans Gmoser gathered at Kluane Lake in the Yukon, their sights set on the east ridge. To make the long approach slightly less onerous, an air drop of supplies was made at the foot of the ridge. In addition, three inflatable life rafts were dropped by the same plane near the terminus of the Donjek Glacier, the source of the Donjek River, just in case fate or chance brought the climbers that way.

Blessed with relatively light packs and travelling on skis, the group reached the supplies and the east ridge only six days after leaving Kluane Lake. They began climbing almost immediately. So strong was this party that only three camps were established above 2,700 metres; and from their high camp at 5,100 metres, with the main difficulties of the ridge behind them, they arrived at the summit of Logan's east peak on June 12th, 1959.

The weather was excellent and the team members far from being played out, so they decided that, rather than simply returning to the lake, they would take a more interesting route back to civilization — a route longer than their approach. Much longer.

Packing their gear together, they went up the Hubbard Glacier and via a tributary reached the head of the Donjek Glacier. They then began to work their way down that vast highway of ice. Due to the approach of the Arctic

The mighty bulk of **Mount Logan**, the highest peak in Canada and one of the most massive mountains in the world.

spring with its rapidly rising daytime temperatures (and rapidly deteriorating snow conditions) they decided to abandon their skis and quite literally "man the lifeboats" and float out down the Donjek River. Accordingly, they set about retrieving the boats that had been airdropped. They found them in a stand of trees, torn to shreds.

More than one hundred patches and many more curses later, the tired climbers clambered warily into their dubious craft and, in the best Canadian tradition, headed down the river. After a series of adventures and more than one near-disaster, the tiny flotilla finally floundered, ignobly enough, on a log-jam a scant three kilometres from the Alaska Highway's Donjek Bridge.

The members of the expedition had travelled more than two hundred and forty kilometres since leaving Kluane Lake and, in the process, had skied, bushwhacked, fallen into crevasses, shivered their way across glaciers, and navigated a treacherous mountain river. And, almost as an aside, they had managed to climb in superb style the highest mountain in the country.

One of the most technically demanding climbs of Logan occurred in 1965 when a party of Californian climbers led by Allen Steck decided to take on the central south ridge, a giddy arête with an overall length of thirteen kilometres. It is a beautiful ridge, but one fraught with danger and difficulties. However, the Steck group succeeded in putting up a magnificent route, and Steck himself also managed to give the ridge a rather charming name.

In the early stages of the climb, while waiting on an airy stance above the Seward Glacier for his turn to advance, Steck heard the telltale whine of a falling rock—the most terrifying note on the alpine scale as far as climbers are concerned. He hugged the ice, flattening himself against the wall so as to present as small a target as possible. He closed his eyes and held his breath. The whining, whirring sound came closer, but it seemed to stay at the same intensity—no Doppler Shift here! Steck opened his eyes, raised his head—and found himself eyeball to eyeball with a hummingbird. Hummingbird Ridge had found a name, and the expedition a friendly, concerned patron.

Ye Gods, Mr. MacCarthy, just look at that; they never will believe we climbed it.

Conrad Kain, on the first ascent of Mount Louis

Named after himself in a fit of vanity by an early hiker, Mount Louis, despite its proximity to Banff, had not been climbed by 1916. Few had even made the attempt, so unlikely seemed the chances of success. It was not until July 15th, 1916, that Conrad Kain and Albert MacCarthy, two members of the Mount Robson first ascent party in 1913, set out on horseback with three others from Banff to enjoy a leisurely Sunday picnic. While munching morsels on a grassy plateau northeast of Louis, Kain and MacCarthy casually assessed the six hundred metres of vertical limestone towering above them. Soon they were skirting the base of the mountain. What had begun as a short after-lunch stroll quickly escalated into a full-fledged attempt up the south face.

Following the line of least resistance, first to the southeast, then to the west, and forcing a final, steep chimney, the two reached the summit of Louis some four hours after beginning their unplanned climb. Although casually undertaken, this first ascent of Louis marked an important breakthrough in Canadian rock climbing. It also served to underscore Kain's position as Canada's premier climber and MacCarthy's reputation as one of the finest amateur climbers of his day in North America.

Today, Louis is one of the most popular rock climbs in the Banff area, with several difficult routes, especially on the south and west faces.

Opposite: **Mount Louis** (8,800 feet/2,682 metres), a popular peak among Banff-area rock climbers.

The manners of mountaineers are commonly savage, but they are rather produced by their situation than derived from their ancestors.

Dr. Samuel Johnson

Mount Lyell straddles the Great Divide, flinging out its five distinct summits, each separated by 150-metre vertical gaps. Peak Four, shown here to the left, rises to 11,160 feet (3,402 metres) and was first climbed via the south ridge in July 1927 by D. Duncan, T. Lynes, Jim Simpson, and Swiss guide Edouard Feuz Jr. Peak Five, at 11,150 feet (3,399 metres), was ascended precisely one year earlier by Feuz and Americans Alfred J. Ostheimer, Dr. Max M. Strumia, and J. Monroe Thorington, via the south ridge.

The clouds had cleared and the night was magnificent, still and starlit. I clipped myself on to the ledge and dozed off. I awoke to find Joe already awake, cursing and shivering in the cold. A point of light on the horizon cheered us up and we watched eagerly for the appearance of the sun. The light grew stronger and we were laughing and talking like normal human beings when suddenly the moon popped up. . . . We spent the rest of the night in utter misery.

Don Whillans, the celebrated British climber

The last rays of a summer day dust the twin spires of **Marmolata** (9,950 feet/3,033 metres) and **Crescent** (9,350 feet/2,850 metres), dominating the centre of Bugaboo Glacier in British Columbia's Purcell Range. Marmolata was first climbed in 1930 by E. Cromwell, Conrad Kain, and Peter Kaufmann via the east ridge. Crescent first fell to J. Monroe Thorington and the remarkable Kain three years later.

There's a land where the mountains are nameless,
And the rivers all run God knows where;
There are lives that are erring and aimless,
And deaths that just hang by a hair;
There are hardships that nobody reckons;
There are valleys unpeopled and still;
There's a land—oh, it beckons and beckons,
And I want to go back—and I will.

Robert W. Service, "The Spell of the Yukon"

Mounts **Moffat** (11,500 feet/3,505 metres), **Samson** (11,000 feet/3,353 metres), and **Hickson** (11,250 feet/3,429 metres), three heavily glaciated peaks all climbed during the course of the Yukon Alpine Centennial Expedition, in July/August 1967.

Completely relaxed, I pulled up on the tiniest of holds with ease and confidence, and the emotional aspect of my situation did not occur to me. I simply thought: "If I fall off here the rope would break and I would fall over a thousand feet clear to the deck."

Lionel Terray, notable French guide

Evening tints the west face of **Neptuak Mountain** (10,620 feet/3,237 metres), or Peak Nine of the famous Ten Peaks ringing Moraine Lake in Banff National Park. Neptuak was first climbed in August 1902 by J. Norman Collie, Hugh Stutfield, G.M. Weed, Herman Wooley, and the guide Christian Kaufmann, via the northwest ridge. The climb was made with all five men on one rope, a practice not especially recommended.

He that mounts the precipices wonders how he came thither and doubts how he shall return. . . . His walk is an adventure and his departure an escape. He has a kind of turbulent pleasure, between fright and admiration.

Dr. Samuel Johnson

The Southern Logan Mountains are a magnificently wild range of peaks tucked away in the Northwest Territories, approximately two hundred and fifty kilometres north of Watson Lake.

Due to the remoteness of these mountains and the often difficult climbing they offer, only a relative handful of parties have been active here. However, thanks to the combination of wild firm rock, vast faces, an exquisite, almost fairyland setting, and charming place names such as Dawnwind Lake, Night-wind Creek, Thunder Dome, and Mount Nirvana, the Southern Logans are destined to become popular among serious mountaineers with a penchant for things wild, remote, technically strenuous, and beautiful.

Opposite: The east face of **Mount Nirvana** in the Southern Logan Range, Northwest Territories.

To climb the trackless mountain all unseen,
  With the wild flock that never needs a fold;
Alone o'er steeps and foaming falls to lean;
  This is not Solitude; 't is but to hold
Converse with Nature's charms, and view her stores unroll'd.

Lord Byron, "Childe Harold"

Below: An outer rampart of the Yukon's **Ogilvie Mountains**, seen from near the Dempster Highway at sunset.

Mountains are good adventure.

Geoffrey Winthrop Young, British mountaineer

Opposite: **Oppy Mountain** (10,840 feet/3,304 metres), seen from a winter camp on the Great Divide's East Alexandra Glacier.

The line which separates the difficult from the dangerous is sometimes very shadowy, but it is not an imaginary line. It is a true line, without breadth. It is often easy to pass, and very hard to see. It is sometimes passed unconsciously, and the consciousness that it has been passed is felt too late. If the doubtful line is crossed consciously, deliberately, one passes from doing that which is justifiable, to doing that which is unjustifiable.

Edward Whymper, first man to climb the Matterhorn

Pigeon Spire was first climbed in August 1930 by E. Cromwell and Peter Kaufmann via the west ridge. However, the most impressive climb done on Pigeon is the route established on the east face in 1960 by Ed Cooper and Layton Kor, two fine rock climbers best known for their ascents in California's Yosemite Valley.

Cooper and Kor found the climbing on the giant slab of granite, which dominates Pigeon's east face, to be demanding but well within their abilities. It was not until they neared the top of the slab that the mountain began to show its teeth:

> The difficulties were beginning in earnest now, as we were approaching the top of the slab, and the angle steepened considerably. Two leads later of free climbing...found us on top of a pedestal admiring the smooth crackless rock above us and yodelling over to some friends on the summit of Snowpatch. This was no time for admiring anything, however, as the clouds were lowering on Pigeon Spire and the Howser Spires were clouded in. Spurred on by this, I dropped down the pedestal on a rope and started swinging. I managed to pendulum over to a crack and after a delicate lead...found a belay spot. The next lead up an inside right corner was also strenuous. Using a piton that sank as I moved up on it, I reached a good handhold that led to easier territory....We reached the summit, 300 feet above, as the first flakes of snow hit us....The rock on this face is excellent, a real joy to climb, and is bound, in the future, to become a classic route.

Opposite: **Pigeon Spire,** at 10,250 feet (3,124 metres), is a delicately carved granitic peak located in British Columbia's Bugaboo Group, a peak characterized by the enormous slab, tilted at an angle of sixty degrees, that dominates the mountain's east face.

"Panguk Pass," as we afterwards called it, is a graceful double curve of snow and ice bounded on the one hand by the broken cliffs of Mt. Barbican, on the other by a lofty buttress of rock jutting out from Mt. Geikie. We walked up the terminal moraine and sat down on a large, ice-borne boulder to put on our crampons. The unfathomable blue of the sky over-arched us; the verdant valley lay below, bathed in the tender light of a youthful day; the soundless voices of the great peaks breathed in our attentive ears; our hearts soared up in an intoxication of happiness.

Cyril G. Wates, describing a climb in the Ramparts, 1926

Opposite above: Sunset over the upper reaches of the **Ramparts** in Jasper National Park.

Opposite below: The **Rampart Massif**, seen here in winter, is located in the vicinity of Jasper's Tonquin Valley and is one of the most impressive clusters of rock in the Canadian Rockies. There is nothing gradualistic about these peaks, no low-lying foothills to prepare the onlooker for the eruption of rock beyond. Instead, the Ramparts leap up in a single wave from idyllic meadows and crystalline lakes and tarns. The dramatic suddenness of these mountains and the beauty of their immediate environs have functioned as a magnet for tourists, hikers, and climbers for decades.

Even in late summer this region looked bleak and utterly desolate, a blotchy brown flatland devoid of life, a vast panorama of emptiness, so bleak and so desolate that it possessed its own unique beauty.

Duncan Pryde, author, adventurer, former fur trader and member of the Northwest Territories Council.

Like a scene from a Western set in Arizona, the **Ram Plateau**, lying in the Mackenzie Mountains of the eastern Northwest Territories, stands solemn guard over a remarkably bleak and remote countryside.

Mt. Resplendent gleaming in the sunlight in front of us, a shining thing and perfectly named. Resplendent, over 11,000 feet high, completely snow-covered and dwarfed in the region only by the mighty 13,000 foot Robson, four miles to the north.

P.L. Pue, on first sight of Mount Resplendent

Below: Like so many other peaks in the vicinity of Mount Robson, **Mount Resplendent** (11,240 feet/3,426 metres) was first climbed by the ubiquitous Austrian Canadian, Conrad Kain, accompanied by the famous mountain photographer, Byron Harmon. They made their ascent in 1911. Often ignored by eager climbers intent on Robson, Resplendent is a strikingly beautiful peak in its own right.

Mountain scenes occupy the same place in our consciousness with remembered melody. It is all one whether I find myself humming the air of some great symphonic movement or gazing upon some particular configuration of rock and snow, of peak and glacier.

George H.L. Mallory, the British climber lost on Everest in 1924

Opposite: Mist and cloud fill nooks, crannies, and valleys in the gently rolling **Richardson Mountains,** skirting the Yukon – Northwest Territories border near the Dempster Highway.

On every side the snowy heads of mighty hills crowded round, whilst immediately behind us, a giant among giants, and immeasurably supreme, rose Robson's peak.

Lord Milton and Walter B. Cheadle, *The North-West Passage by Land*

Perhaps no other peak in Canada so dominates its setting as does Mount Robson (12,972 feet/3,954 metres) in eastern British Columbia. Its steeply turreted ridges, mazelike icefalls, featureless faces, tremendous base-to-summit height, and sheer bulk make this much more than simply the highest mountain in the Canadian Rockies. Robson is a frozen, primeval force, a vast eruption of earth and ice shaped into one of the great mountains of the world.

Before the coming of the European, Robson was known as *Yuh-hai-has-kun,* or "Mountain of the Spiral Road," due to the distinctive horizontal banding sometimes visible on the upper reaches of the peak. Its ridges often draped in cloud, its slopes regularly wracked by avalanche, from its first recorded encounter with Europeans in 1827 until 1913, Robson remained unclimbed—and, in the minds of many, unclimbable.

However, some mountaineers disagreed. Among them was one Reverend George Kinney, who was a member of the first party to reconnoitre Robson's immediate environs in 1907. From that first brief encounter, Kinney became obsessed with the notion that he should be the first person to stand on the mountain's summit. Obsession turned to near-frenzy in 1909, when Kinney, in Edmonton during the early summer, caught wind of the news that a strong party was heading for "his" peak. Wasting no time, he set out on his own from the Alberta capital, convinced that he would find an appropriate climbing companion along the way.

Kinney's faith was vindicated. Circumstance (or was it divine intervention?) in the form of a flood-swollen river brought the Reverend together with the rather gullible but strong-backed D. "Curlie" Phillips, trapper, outfitter, and still slightly wet-behind-the-ears mountain man. Stranded together on the same bank of the river, the intense Kinney and the gregarious Phillips immediately hit it off. Kinney was a most persuasive man, as befitted one of his calling, and he soon had the unfortunate Phillips convinced that there was absolutely nothing else in the world he would rather do than throw in his lot with the lone preacher and attempt to climb one of the most forboding—and feared—mountains in the Rockies.

After numerous adventures, the couple eventually arrived safely at Berg Lake, snuggled up against the lap of Robson. Kinney, never at a loss for words, later described the setting:

> From where we camped, Mt. Robson rose in one sheer unbroken wall from base to highest summit, and at such a fearful angle that a snow cornice, breaking off the crest, would fall seven thousand feet before it could come to a stop.

The two immediately set about ferrying up equipment and also food, of which they had very little (thanks in part to a gun with a crooked barrel!) to a point high above the camp at Berg Lake in order to establish an advance base. This task completed, it was simply a question of waiting for a break in the stormy weather, which precluded all climbing—or of waiting until their food finally ran out.

When it looked as if the latter was going to happen well before the former,

Previous spread:
Approaching the summit cornice, "whipped-cream roll" on **Robson's** north face.

From the summit of **Robson**, Conrad Kain gazed spellbound at the view: "Glorious in all directions. One could compare the sea of glaciers and mountains with a stormy ocean. Mt. Robson is about 2,000 feet higher than all the other mountains in the neighbourhood. Indescribably beautiful was the vertical view towards Berg Lake."

they launched a desperate assault, struggling upward under extremely poor conditions:

> On all that upper climb we did nearly the whole work on our toes and hands only. The clouds were a blessing in a way, for they shut out the view of the fearful depths below. A single slip meant a slide to death. At times the storm was so thick that we could see but a few yards, and the sleet would cut at our faces and nearly blind us. Our clothes and hair were one frozen mass of snow and ice.

Despite all this, and despite the almost complete inexperience of Curlie Phillips, the two continued to gain ground. Then, suddenly, they were up, as Kinney described:

> "Give me your hand, Curlie." "I'll give you my sock," says Curlie. Thrusting into my mittened hand his gloved one, over which he had pulled a woolen sock for better warmth, Donald Phillips and I congratulated each other on at last succeeding in capturing that most difficult peak, Mt. Robson. We stood on the needle point of the highest and finest peak of all the Canadian Rockies, and the day was Friday, August the thirteenth, 1909. . . .
> Baring my head I said: "In the name of Almighty God, by whose strength I have climbed here, I capture this peak, Mt. Robson, for my own country, and for the Alpine Club of Canada."

God, country, club, and conquest. There was only one problem. They hadn't reached the top.

Although they had climbed to a point quite near the summit, they had been forced to turn back because of the fierce storm that buffeted them. Yet apparently they had agreed that "almost" was good enough. So, in spite of the widespread acclaim that greeted the two climbers upon their return, one simple fact remained: Robson had still not been climbed to the very top.

It finally happened four years later. Fittingly enough, the man who led the successful party was the greatest mountaineer in the annals of alpinism in Canada — the Austrian-born, naturalized Canadian guide, Conrad Kain.

On July 31st, 1913, with British Columbia's deputy minister of public works, Mr. W.W. ("Bill") Foster, and the American climber Albert MacCarthy (from, of all places, Alpine, New Jersey!), Kain reached the summit of Robson via the east face and the southeast ridge. Leading all the way, he was forced to chop thousands of steps in armourlike glare ice. His companions followed, balancing precariously on tiny holds, with fierce winds threatening to rip them off the side of the mountain at any moment. Whenever the issue seemed in doubt, Kain came through magnificently. Grudgingly, Robson revealed its secrets to him until he, MacCarthy, and Foster finally reached the summit that had eluded Kinney and Phillips. Robson had been climbed.

A climber approaches the summit of **Mount Robson**, at 12,972 feet (3,954 metres) the highest peak in the Canadian Rockies. "The wind here was so bad," wrote Conrad Kain, when describing his own ascent, "that I often had to stop. The steepness alone, apart from the wind, made step-cutting very hard work. For a number of steps I first had to make a handhold in the ice, and swing the axe with one hand."

Opposite: **Mount Robson** at midday, with the Emperor Ridge on the right skyline and Tumbling Glacier in the foreground.

Sun slanting off the icy ramp of **Mount Robson's** northwest face.

Since that first successful ascent, many new and challenging routes have been established. Most notable among these, and all pioneered by American teams, were: the 1958 ascent of the extremely long and complex Wishbone Arête by Don Claunch, Harvey Firestone, and Mike Sherrick; Ron Perla and Tom Spencer's successful route up the spectacular Emperor Ridge in 1961; and, perhaps most impressive of all, the first ascent of Robson's awesome north face, one of the finest ice climbs in North America, by Pat Callis and Dan Davis, also in 1961.

While mountaineers from all over the world flock to Robson each year in ever-increasing numbers, a climb of the mountain from any of its ridges or faces remains a serious undertaking. Those who would approach *Yuh-hai-has-kun* lightly are often cruelly rebuffed. This great mountain growlingly relents only to those whose spirit, skill, courage, and luck match its own elemental power and brute strength.

A stupendous rock!

Ross Cox, on first view of Roche Miette, 1817

Roche Miette (7,599 feet/2,316 metres), the rocky guardian of the eastern battlements of Jasper National Park.

June 27. Remained on a small plain in the mountains in some pine trees. Grass near the river & the horses were there for some time. There were only three of us. We had prayers twice & I read. It was most interesting to me to be quite among the mountains & a time never to be forgotten. The scenery is most magnificient. The first Sunday I have spent in the mountains.

The Reverend Robert T. Rundle, for whom the mountain was named

Mount Rundle (9,675 feet/2,949 metres), in actuality a striking ridge with seven distinct summits, is quite possibly the most photographed mountain in Canada, thanks to its close proximity to the town of Banff.

It was named for the Reverend Robert Terrill Rundle, a Wesleyan missionary dispatched from England in 1840, with the blessings of the Hudson's Bay Company, to bring enlightenment to the native people west of Lake Superior.

The name first appeared officially in 1863. Local tradition had it that Robert Rundle was the first white man to visit the site of what is now Banff, camping just below Cascade Mountain, but although he did indeed visit the area in 1847, there seems little doubt that Governor George Simpson of the Hudson's Bay Company was in fact there first, as early as 1841. Be that as it may, the much-admired mountain's namesake was thrown from a horse, severely injuring his left arm, the year of his visit to the Banff area; as a consequence, he returned to England in early 1848. He died at Garstang, Lancashire, in 1896 at the ripe old age of eighty-five, probably completely oblivious of the fact that ten thousand kilometres away his name had become virtually a household word.

Mount Rundle was first climbed in 1888 by J.J. McArthur. While it is quite possible simply to stroll to the summit, there are also some extremely challenging rock routes to be found, especially on the eastern end of the massif.

Opposite: **Mount Rundle** — the classic view.

"What do you seek friends?

Know you not that the valleys hold
Wealth of silver and wealth of gold?"
'Yes but the mountains which seem so bare
Have burden of treasure more rich and rare
    Than any you know.'

"What treasures are these friends?"

'The winds of God are more than wealth,
For they tint the cheek with the glow of health,
And the pulses throbbing in every vein
Give a sense of joy that is almost pain
    To the thrilling heart.'

Cyril G. Wates, prominent member of the Canadian Alpine Club in the twenties and thirties

Opposite: Also known as **Sapta**, Peak Five (10,010 feet/3,051 metres), lowest of the Ten Peaks of Banff's Moraine Lake area, appears little more than a satellite of nearby Mount Allen (Peak Six) when viewed from a distance. While some doubt exists as to the actual date of the first ascent, the first verifiable climb of Peak Five was made in 1927 by the Herman Ulrichs party, via the south ridge.

Tired? Of course. Exhausted? By no means. Happy? Only those who hold in memory the retrospect of such a day can know the feeling.

Frank Freeborn, on reaching the summit of Mount Sir Donald

Mount Sir Donald (10,818 feet/3,297 metres) has long served as a beacon to climbers, dominating as it does the Rogers Pass area of British Columbia's Selkirk Range.

From the year of its first ascent in 1890 by the Swiss guides Huber and Sulzer, Sir Donald became an extremely popular climb, thanks in no small part to its proximity to what was at the turn of the century the Alpine Mecca of Canada—Glacier House, the beautiful mountain lodge constructed by the Canadian Pacific Railway to attract tourists to the mountains through which its rail line ran.

While Sir Donald was undeniably an attractive target, it was not often climbed in the early days. Frank Freeborn, one of the first to make it to the top in one piece, put it this way:

> In actual height it is overtopped by some mountains that are oftener climbed, but in elevation above any convenient starting point it considerably surpasses them. Add to this fact its excessive steepness, the difficulty of crossing its bergschrund, and the danger from falling rock, and you have the explanation of the infrequency of its ascent.

Of the many fine ascents that have been made on Sir Donald over the years, the incredibly swift and elegant climb of the north face in 1961 by the remarkable American climbers Fred Beckey and Yvon Chouinard stands out. This impressive high-angle face rises a full eight hundred metres from the Uto Glacier, yet Beckey and Chouinard, certainly two of the finest climbers on this continent in this century, finished off the climb, over entirely virgin terrain, in a scant five hours.

Writing later of the ascent, Beckey noted that, in retrospect, "at a normal pace and with as much protection as one would use for a comparable, but much shorter face, it seems doubtful that one could complete the climb in one day." Such understatement is worthy of Louis Lachenal—the agile French climber who was so matter-of-fact about his incredible ascents.

Opposite: **Mount Sir Donald,** one of the most dramatic mountains in the Selkirks, is viewed here from the Rogers Pass area.

Burgener at this point exhibited most painful anxiety, and his "Herr Gott! geben Sie Acht!" had the very ring of tears in its earnest entreaty. On my emergence into daylight his anxiety was explained. Was not the knapsack on my shoulders, and were not sundry half-bottles of Bonvier in the knapsack?

Albert F. Mummery, nineteenth-century British rock climber

Opposite: **Mount Sir Douglas** (11,174 feet/3,406 metres), the highest peak between the Palliser and North Kananaskis passes, was first climbed in August 1919 by J. Hickson and E. Ferry via the west ridge. This view is of its northwest face.

Huge as the tower which builders vain
Presumptuous piled on Shimar's plain,
The rocky summits, split and rent,
Formed turret, dome, or battlement,
Or seemed fantastically set
With cupola or minaret.

Sir Walter Scott

Above: **Snowpatch Spire,** reflecting the last rays of sun before dusk.

Snowpatch Spire (10,050 feet/3,063 metres) is an appropriately named upthrust of compact granite, the last of the major summits of the Bugaboo Group to be climbed. It was not until August 1940 that the south summit was reached by Canadian Jack Arnold and American Raffi Bedayn, via a route beginning to the left, then extending directly above the prominent snow field on the east face from which the peak derives its name.

The key pitch of the first ascent presented itself some four rope lengths below the top:

> On a very smooth, vertical face and, running upwards across the face at a seventy degree tangent, was a quartz vein with small knobs protruding. None of these knobs extended more than an inch and most of them considerably less. Raffi, placing pitons in the vein, led up on these small knobs, to where he was stopped by a large overhang. This necessitated a traverse to the left, purely on the arms, to the base of a large chock-stone where this pitch ends. On following, I found the balance on these knobs very critical and the arm traverse so difficult, due to the character of the sloping hold, that the only way I could get adequate purchase was to balance with my right fore-arm and, with the left hand helping, inch my way across. The entire pitch is done under extreme exposure and I dare say the next party will find it interesting indeed.

Opposite: Massive **Snowpatch Spire,** one of the dominant peaks of the Bugaboo Group, seen from the shores of a small glacial tarn.

Escape was impossible; we were directly in the path of the slide, and could only stand and face what seemed certain destruction. Death hovered close, his eyes kind, his breath singularly fragrant; fear withdrew to an immeasurable distance.

Cyril G. Wates, describing his experience in an avalanche

Edward Whymper, the first man to climb Switzerland's Matterhorn in 1865 (an ascent shrouded in controversy due to the deaths of several members of the party during the descent), was also the first to climb Mount Stanley. He went up via the northwest ridge in 1901, accompanied by four Swiss guides.

Sixty-five years later, the ubiquitous guide Hans Kahl and his partner Nick Ellens established a new route up Stanley, via the prominent snow and ice sections of the east face. In climbing the longest snow/ice route in the Rockies, excluding the longer routes on Mount Robson, the two climbers were forced to struggle up steep, soft snow in the upper third of the face. The snow was so treacherous that a fall could not have been stopped if either of them had lost their footing.

Opposite: At 10,351 feet (3,155 metres), **Mount Stanley** is one of the dominant peaks in the Ball Range of eastern British Columbia. Its east face, seen here looking deceptively tranquil, is a very dangerous climb.

A popular misconception of climbing is that it requires great strength and nerve. If that were true then the strongest men would be the best climbers, which is not so. Strength is obviously an asset to a climber, but the most important thing is a combination of the mental ability to work out technical problems, physical suppleness and agility and the right amount of confidence.

Joe Brown, veteran British climber

Mount Steele (16,644 feet/5,073 metres) is one of the principal peaks of the St. Elias Mountains, the vast range of mighty summits that straddle the Yukon-Alaska border, forming the roof of North America. Steele is connected with nearby Lucania Mountain via a 4,200-metre-high saddle. A climb of the one is often combined with a climb of the other.

Mensch, ist das wunderbar! *Right in front of me, wonderful in the evening sun, shone the hanging glacier of Mt. Temple. Like a fairyland, glittered in an unforgettable blue, its many crevasses, its virgin snow-blanket.*

Hans Wittich, during the first ascent of the east ridge of Mount Temple, 1932

Banff's hulking **Mount Temple,** brooding over Paradise Valley.

Mount Temple (11,626 feet/3,544 metres) is a hulking, misshapen giant, totally dominating the Lake Louise area. Its heavily towered east ridge, like the ruins of a once-mighty, now shattered Keep, crumbles down to the patiently waiting waters of Moraine Lake.

Seen from the north, ice and snow rather than weather and time-blasted rock seem the stuff of Temple. Its massive icecap casts off dazzling rays of light and terrifyingly destructive avalanches with equal ease. Seen from any angle, whether shrouded in wind-torn rags of mist or standing out against a brilliant azure backdrop, Temple is an impressive mountain.

The first serious attempt to climb it was made in the summer of 1893 by Walter Wilcox and Samuel Allen, both American college students. This

attempt, from the north, was eventually halted at the 3,200-metre level by a 120-metre-high vertical wall, apparently devoid of handholds. The two disappointed climbers were forced to return to their base camp at Lake Louise, which at the time was "little more than a muskeg filled with mosquitoes and tree stumps."

The next year Wilcox and Allen returned, determined to succeed this time. Striking out from the floor of Paradise Valley, together with a third climber, L. Frissell, they reached windy Sentinel Pass, so named by Allen for a pinnacle "standing at the crest of the Pass like a lone watchman." (See photo of the Grand Sentinel.) From Sentinel Pass, the way to the summit was assured. Slowly ascending seemingly endless scree slopes and scaling the occasional band of cliffs, the three climbers reached the top without incident on August 17th, 1894. The easiest path to the summit had been discovered. Far more difficult routes remained to be conceived—and climbed.

In 1932, Hans Wittich and Otto Stegmaier placed a fine route up the long and strenuous east ridge. Wittich's description of the final stages of the climb bears repeating:

> The ice-ridge was now cruelly steep, and sharp as a knife. Otto hewed the steps for a while on the glacier side of the ice ridge. Soon we reached the limit. If only we had crampons, then it would be easy . . . . I traversed very carefully and then went up to the top of the nose, step by step. The summit at last! But, by the devil, this was not the summit! . . . Then, like a demon, I swung the ice-axe; we must reach it before complete darkness. At 8:30 P.M. we clasped hands. Far in the west, a last dark red glow; down in the valleys night had fallen.

Over the intervening forty-odd years, many new and challenging routes have been placed on Temple's ridges and faces, such as Art Gran and John Hudson's fine ascent via the right side of the southeast face in 1962. Temple's reputation as one of the most challenging alpine massifs in the Rockies, when combined with its ease of access, makes it an extremely popular Canadian climbing goal.

I commanded the chief guide to arrange the men and animals in single file, twelve feet apart, and lash them all together on a strong rope. He objected that the first two miles was a dead level, with plenty of room, and that the rope was never used except in very dangerous places. But I would not listen to that. My reading had taught me that many serious accidents had happened. . .simply from not having the people tied up soon enough. . . .

When the procession stood at ease, roped together and ready to move, I never saw a finer sight. It was 3,122 feet long—over half a mile; every man but Harris and me was on foot, and had on his green veil and his blue goggles and his white rag around his hat, and his coil of rope over one shoulder and under the other, and his ice axe in his belt, and carried his alpenstock in his left hand, his umbrella (closed) in his right, and his crutches slung at his back.

Mark Twain, setting out for the restaurant on top of the Riffelberg

Sunset over the **Tombstone Range**, in the Yukon Territory's Ogilvie Mountains. Talus Lake lies in the foreground.

Many mountains are rounded, old, and tired, geological dullards standing out only because the surrounding landscape is, by comparison, duller still. Some peaks, however, juxtaposing rock and air in delicate symmetry, excite both the eye and the spirit.

These are the stone needles. Sharp, acrid, uncompromising, they thrust themselves upward in shocking spurts. Lovely, their rock often lacelike, yet terrifying in their rocky verticality, these mountains are the substance of both dream and nightmare. The mountains of the Tombstone Range are such peaks.

The Monolith, a major peak
in the Tombstone Range,
Yukon Territory.

Overleaf: **The Monolith** seen
from close range.

Above: Looking more like a setting in the Ruwenzori Range than something one would expect to find in Canada, a peak rises from the mists near **Upper Victoria Lake** on Moresby Island in the Queen Charlottes.

When about five miles from the Nsabé Camp. . .my eyes were directed by a boy to a mountain said to be covered with salt, and I saw a peculiar cloud of a most beautiful silver colour, which assumed the proportions and appearance of a vast mountain covered with snow. Following its form downward I became struck with the deep blue-black colour of its base, and wondered if it portended another tornado; then as the sight descended to the gap between the eastern and western plateaus, I became for the first time conscious that what I gazed upon was not the image or semblance of a vast mountain, but the solid substance of a real one, with its summit covered with snow. I ordered a halt and examined it carefully with a field-glass, then took a compass bearing of the centre of it, and found it bear 215 magnetic. It now dawned upon me that this must be the Ruwenzori.

Henry Morton Stanley, *In Darkest Africa*

No mountain is worth as much as one's life.

Walter Bonatti, celebrated Italian climber

Here, **Mount Vancouver** is seen punching its way through a few wisps of cloud high above the Hubbard Glacier in the St. Elias Mountains.

Mount Vancouver (15,860 feet/4,834 metres), a major peak located squarely on the border between Alaska and the Yukon in the St. Elias Mountains, is a mountain with two distinct summits. So distinct are they that each has its own name. Vancouver's North Peak was considered the only major high point on the mountain until, in 1948, Dr. Walter Wood of Arlington, Virginia, showed that the South Peak was nothing to sneeze at, standing a full 15,720 feet (4,791 metres) above sea level.

The higher northern summit was first climbed by Noel Odell and his party in 1949. In 1967, the southern summit was chosen as a suitable goal for a joint Canadian-American expedition. As the term "South Peak of Mount Vancouver" somehow lacked the exuberantly self-conscious self-assuredness that earmarked the Canadian Centennial, it was dubbed, almost inevitably, "Good Neighbour Peak."

The upper reaches of **Mount Victoria's** east face, scene of one of the most tragic mountaineering accidents in Canadian climbing history.

Und willst du die schlafende Löwin nicht wecken
So wandre still durch die Strasse der Schrecken.
(And if the sleeping lions you would not waken in the night
Then tread ever so lightly along the street of fright.)

J.C. Friedrich von Schiller

Mount Victoria (south summit: 11,365 feet/3,464 metres; north summit: 11,116 feet/3,388 metres) must rank as one of the classic peaks of Canada. Classic because of its setting, sweeping high as it does above Lake Louise. Classic, too, in that it was first ascended during the initial heyday of Canadian alpinism by a party which included the brilliant British chemist and mountaineer, J. Norman Collie, as well as Peter Sarbach, one of the finest Swiss guides of his day and the first of his number to climb in Canada.

Collie's party, fresh from the previous day's first ascent of nearby Mount Lefroy, moved quickly from the chalet at Lake Louise to the col at the top of Abbot's Pass, via what has become known as the Death Trap, a steep, narrow snow slope prone to frequent avalanching.

From Abbot's Pass, the route to Victoria's summit was straightforward: one slogging foot after the other in the soft, heavy snow until the peak was climbed. After thirty minutes of photography, sightseeing, and sunbathing on the top, the climbers retraced their steps. A quick romp down the Death Trap and a hard pull across the lake in the intrepid rowboat *Agnes* brought them back to the bosom of civilization, in the form of the chalet, and, more particularly, to the steaks and coffee of Mr. Howard, the much-acclaimed resident chef.

Since that first climb in 1897, thousands have reached Victoria's twin summits. Most have dutifully followed in Collie's footsteps. Others have put up new routes of greater difficulty. For all its beauty, its stunning setting, and its popularity among climbers, Victoria is perhaps best known not for the many who have succeeded in reaching its summits, but for those few who have failed — at the cost of their lives.

On July 30th, 1954, one of the worst accidents in the history of Canadian mountaineering occurred on Mount Victoria. On that day, seven climbers from Mexico — six women and a male guide — set out from the hut at Abbot's Pass for the south summit. Rather than following Collie's route up the southeast ridge, the Mexicans forced a path straight up the east face. The party climbed linked together with two ropes — three women and their guide on one, the remaining three women on the other.

There was a thick layer of snow on Victoria that year, and it was solid early in the morning. The climbers were easily able to kick secure steps, and they reached the top quite early. But at noon, when they decided to descend, they made a fatal mistake. By this time the sun had begun to warm the snow slabs on the east face, making the outer layer of snow extremely unstable and prone to sliding. Basic climbing sense should have dictated a dull but safe trudge down the easy rock of the southeast ridge, but the Mexicans chose to head down — straight down — the treacherous east face.

Only a short distance below the south summit, one of the climbers on the lead rope slipped. She quickly gathered speed. The others were unable to stop her, and they in turn were tugged, one by one, from their stances and hurled headlong down the steep snow, crashing into the rock buttresses below before being tossed out into a high arc onto the steep snows of the Death Trap. The four came to rest more than six hundred metres below the point of the first climber's slip. They were all dead.

The three remaining women stayed on the east face, shocked and completely immobilized by the fate of their comrades. A rescue party helped them off the mountain over twelve hours later, numbed with grief, half-frozen from crouching motionless on tiny stances hacked out of the unstable snow. Seven had climbed up, full of life and enthusiasm. Only three climbed down, their lives utterly changed. Victoria, unnoticing and uncaring, continued to gaze serenely down upon Lake Louise.

Play for more than you can afford to lose, and you will learn the game.

Sir Winston Churchill

The south face of **The Wedge** (9,484 feet/2,891 metres), a major peak in the relatively unknown Valhalla Range of British Columbia's rugged southern Selkirk Mountains.

With us Nature has been too generous. Man will settle in our valleys and the mountains will be near them in many ways, but with our scientific spirit and our modern efficiency we shall proceed to tear the heart out of the mystery, our mountains will doubtless be minutely classified as to their geological constituents and as to all phenomena connected with them, but by that time men will have ceased to look for them as a blessing at the bottom of the wine cup and to sigh to be entombed in one of them as a guarantee of life hereafter.

Sir Edmund Walker, Honorary President of the Alpine Club of Canada, 1917

Looking southeast from a ridge above the southern end of Lake Gillespie in the central Yukon's desolate **Wernecke Mountains.**

An artist is superior to an unlearned picture-seer, not merely because he has greater natural sensibility, but because he has improved it by methodical experience; because his senses have been sharpened by constant practice, till he can catch finer shades of colouring, and more delicate inflexions of line; because, also, the lines and colour have acquired new significance, thoughts with which the mass of mankind has never cared to connect them. The mountaineer is improved by a similar process.

Leslie Stephen, nineteenth-century climber

Whitehorn Mountain (11,139 feet/3,395 metres), located approximately eight and a half kilometres west-northwest of Mount Robson, was first climbed in August 1911 by Conrad Kain, the indefatigable Austrian-Canadian mountaineer. The left skyline seen here is the southeast ridge; the north ridge and northwest face are on the right.

This open-air life suits me well, though, when one considers it bit by bit, it does not seem so very charming. Long wearisome riding, indifferent monotonous eating, no sport to speak of, hard bed upon the ground, hot sun, wet, no companion of my own class; nevertheless I am happier than I have been for years.

James Carnegie, Earl of Southesk

Looking down into the **Wokkpash Lake** drainage in the Mount Roosevelt – Churchill Peak – Stalin Peak area of north-central British Columbia. This region is extremely remote, and while the climbing afforded is not of an especially high standard, the views from the higher peaks are truly spectacular.

I'm finished.

Toni Kurz

His last words, uttered while quite literally dangling at the end of his rope after a terrible accident on Switzerland's Eiger north face. With all his companions dead, young Kurz was trapped for over two days on the unclimbed face, buffeted by hurricane-velocity winds, wracked with bitter cold. A rescue party of local guides came as close to his stance as possible, then urged him to rope down to them—and safety. But Kurz had no rope. So, with one hand completely frozen, he chopped away bits of rope from the bodies of his comrades and, using his teeth, unravelled the pieces, splicing them together into a line long enough to reach the guides. This unbelievable task, done with his one usable hand while clinging to tiny holds on the most forbidding face in the Alps, took five long hours. By means of the line, Kurz managed to haul up a rope from the guides, which he used to descend to their position. When within centimetres of rescue, a knot in the rope jammed against his carabiner. He hadn't the strength to force it through. So there, finally, the young climber's will to live ebbed out. Toni Kurz died before the eyes and almost within the grasp of the hardened, mountain-wise guides who had hoped to save him. Standing on their small ledge overhanging the abyss, the storm seemed to recede about them. They wept uncontrollably.

Overleaf: Mount John Laurie, more popularly known as **Yamnuska** (7,890 feet/2,405 metres), is quite possibly the most-climbed piece of real estate in Canada. The grey limestone of its east face, located fifty kilometres east of Banff, presents a familiar view to travellers whipping by in their cars on the Trans-Canada, heading for the coast from Calgary. Most climbs on Yamnuska graduate from steep to downright overhanging. Here John Calvert, appropriately clad, contemplates his partner on Yamnuska's "Red Shirt."

Glossary

ARÊTE   Quite simply, a narrow ridge.

BELAY   To anchor or secure fellow climbers, using a rope and other equipment, depending on the situation and the terrain. An absolutely vital technique which a surprising number of climbers do not adequately master. The result: unnecessary accidents.

BERGSCHRUND   The gap, often both deep and wide, separating a glacier from abutting steep rock and/or ice.

CARABINER   An oval or D-shaped metal device with a spring gate. Used in conjunction with pitons, ice screws, chockstones and expansion bolts to protect the climber and to assist in direct aid climbing.

CHOCKSTONE (CHOCK, NUT)   A rock jammed in a crack or chimney which, depending on its placement, may make a move easier or more difficult for the climber. Inspired by the natural chockstone, metal "chocks" or "jam nuts" are fast overtaking pitons as protective and artificial aid devices.

COL   A depression in a mountain ridge.

CRAMPONS   A hinged or rigid set of metal spikes strapped to the climber's boots. Crampons make climbing on steep, firm snow and ice a good deal easier.

DIRECT AID   A general term used to denote any form of climbing in which upward progress is achieved with the use of mechanical devices.

EXPANSION BOLTS   Developed in the United States in the late 1940s to make possible ascents of absolutely holdless rock walls. A hole is drilled in the rock, a bolt is inserted into the hole, then a "hanger" is screwed onto the bolt, through which a carabiner may be clipped as with a piton. As bolts quite drastically alter the rock and change completely both the character and degree of difficulty of a climb, their use is generally frowned upon by the new wave of eco-climbers.

FREE CLIMBING   The opposite of direct aid climbing. That is, any form of climbing in which upward progress is achieved without the use of mechanical devices.

GENDARME   A rock tower straddling a ridge, making forward progress difficult, sometimes impossible.

ICEFALL   An especially steep section of glacier, characterized by deep crevasses and high, often unstable ice towers (seracs). An icefall is to a glacier what a rapid is to a river.

ICE SCREW   A solid or tubular threaded metal alloy device with a pointed tip usually pounded (or tapped), then screwed into hard ice. Serves the same purpose as a piton on rock.

MASSIF   A compact group of mountain peaks or high points.

MORAINE   Rocky debris scoured out of the mountainside by glacial action, deposited at the furthest point of the glacier's advance. Slogging up the side of a steep moraine on a hot day carrying a heavy pack is not one of the most pleasant aspects of mountaineering.

PITON   A metal spike or wedge with an eye. When pounded into a suitably sized crack, a carabiner is clipped through the eye, the rope through the carabiner. This piton-carabiner-rope system may be used as a protective arrangement or to facilitate direct-aid climbing. When handled properly, piton placement becomes a creative art. When abused or done without skill and discretion, pitons may in fact destroy the adjacent rock to such an extent as to alter the nature of a climb completely. It is partly for this reason that more and more climbers in Canada and elsewhere are turning to the use of "chocks" as an attractive alternative to pitons.

TALUS   A sloping mass of rock fragments found immediately below a cliff.

TAMP-IN   An ancient American slang term for an expansion bolt.

TARN   A small high-mountain lake.

TRAVERSE   To proceed around, rather than straight over the top of an obstacle.

VERGLAS   A thin coating of often very hard ice covering rock.

WHITE-OUT   A common condition experienced especially on glaciers and snow slopes when low cloud and fog merge with the white surface, making it extremely difficult to judge depth and distance. Depending on the circumstances, white-outs can be extremely dangerous.

Selected Bibliography

Baird, David M.   *Banff National Park*.   Edmonton: Hurtig Publishers, 1977.
_____.   *Jasper National Park*.   Edmonton: Hurtig Publishers, 1977.
Bonatti, Walter.   *The Great Days*.   London: Victor Gollancz Ltd., 1974.
Bonnington, Christian.   *Annapurna, South Face*.   London: Cassell, 1971.

Brown, Joe. *The Hard Years: The Autobiography of Joe Brown.* London: Victor Gollancz Ltd., 1967.

Fraser, Esther. *The Canadian Rockies: Early Travels and Explorations.* Edmonton: Hurtig Publishers, 1969.

Gillman, Peter and Haston, Dougal. *Eiger Direct.* London: Collins, 1966.

Harrer, Heinrich. *The White Spider: The History of the Eiger's North Face.* London: Rupert Hart-Davis, 1965.

Herrligkoffer, Dr. Karl. *Nanga Parbat.* Toronto: Ryerson Press, 1954.

Hornbein, Thomas F. *Everest: The West Ridge.* New York: Sierra Club and Ballantine Books, 1966.

Hunt, Sir John. *The Ascent of Everest.* London: Hodder & Stoughton, 1953.

Jones, Chris. *Climbing in North America.* Berkeley: University of California Press, 1976.

Kruszyna, Robert and Putnam, William L. *Climber's Guide to the Interior Ranges of British Columbia (South).* Springfield, Mass.: The American Alpine Club and The Alpine Club of Canada, 1977.

Morin, Nea. *A Woman's Reach: Mountaineering Memoirs.* London: Eyre & Spottiswoode, 1968.

Munday, Don. *The Unknown Mountain.* London: Hodder & Stoughton, 1948 (reprinted by The Mountaineers, Seattle, 1975).

Noyce, Wilfrid. *South Col.* London: William Heinemann Ltd., 1954.

Putnam, William L. *Climber's Guide to the Interior Ranges of British Columbia (North).* Springfield, Mass.: The American Alpine Club and The Alpine Club of Canada, 1975.

Putnam, William L. and Boles, Glen W. *Climber's Guide to the Rocky Mountains of Canada (South).* Springfield, Mass.: The American Alpine Club and The Alpine Club of Canada, 1974.

Putnam, William L. and Jones, Chris. *Climber's Guide to the Rocky Mountains of Canada (North).* Springfield, Mass.: The American Alpine Club and The Alpine Club of Canada, 1974.

Rébuffat, Gaston. *Men and the Matterhorn.* New York: Oxford University Press, 1967.

_____. *On Snow and Rock.* London: Nicholas Vane, 1966.

Robbins, Royal. *Basic Rockcraft.* Glendale, California: La Siesta Press, 1971.

Roberts, David. *The Mountain of My Fear.* New York: Vanguard Press, 1968.

Russell, Andy. *The Rockies.* Edmonton: Hurtig Publishers, 1974.

Sherman, Paddy. *Cloud Walkers.* Toronto: Macmillan of Canada Ltd., 1965.

Smythe, Frank S. *Climbs in the Canadian Rockies.* New York: Norton & Co., 1951.

Taylor, William C. *The Snows of Yesteryear: J. Norman Collie, Mountaineer.* Toronto: Holt, Rinehart and Winston of Canada Ltd., 1973.

Terray, Lionel and Ormerod, Alick. *Conquistadors of the Useless.* London: Victor Gollancz, 1963.

Whillans, Don. *Don Whillans: Portrait of a Mountaineer.* London: William Heinemann Ltd., 1971.

Journals:

The Alpine Journal.
The American Alpine Journal.
The Canadian Alpine Journal.

Picture Credits

Rob Ashburner, 23, 27 upper, 31, 32, 35, 51, 60, 65, 90, 93, 97, 98, 101 lower, 116, 135

Paul von Baich/The Image Bank of Canada, 47, 96

David Bedry, 95

Don Beers, 25, 44, 53, 66, 69, 82, 91, 92, 104, 112, 122, 124, 126, 127, 128, 139

John Bingham, 105, 130, 131, 132

Glen Boles, 22, 27 lower, 36, 42, 50, 55, 63, 71, 86, 120

J. David Denning, 109, 110

Hans Fuhrer, 17, 19, 28, 40/41, 59, 70, 76, 79, 101 upper, 113, 119, 134

Janet Green/The Image Bank of Canada, 85

Greg Horne, 34, 61

D.G. Horton, 102, 133, 138

Raymond Jotterand, 106/107

Dan Jurak, 30, 88/89, 111

Janis Kraulis/The Image Bank of Canada, 80

S.J. Krasemann, 33, 43, 49, 103, 121

J.A. Lamont, 21, 37

Keith McDougall, 24, 74

Patrick Morrow, 137

Marianne Morse, 72/73

Wilhelm Schmidt, 123

Wilf Schurig, 46, 56/57

Chic Scott, 18, 45, 52, 142

E. Sian, 115

D.H. Vitt, 75, 140

Editorial / Carlotta Lemieux
Design & Production / David Shaw
Composition / ATTIC typesetting
Separations / Empress Litho Plate Limited
Printing / York Litho Limited
Binding / Hunter Rose Company